Cyberbullying

Strategies to battle the hidden threat to today's school children

S. M. CARLSON

Cyberbullying.

For information, contact: S. M. Carlson 18 2nd Street, Luray, VA 22835.

This book may be purchased for educational, business, or sales promotional use. For information, please email sales@stockNum.com.

www.SMCarlson.com

First Edition

ISBN: 978-1-7336755-2-9 (paperback)

Also by the same author

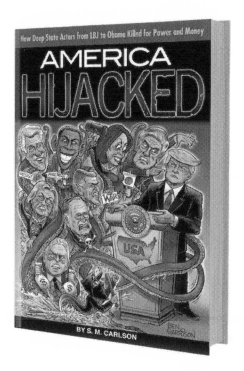

America Hijacked is a thought-provoking analysis that spans both the political right and left and how both the Bush and Clinton families profited from the destruction of the American Dream.

Written shortly and concisely and is easily approachable to all readers.

Available in paperback, hardcover, eBook and Audible audio formats.

www.AmericaHijackedBook.com

www.SMCarlson.com

Cyberbully.watch is a service created by the author of this book. Parents and educators can use our tool for free to search our database of more than 100 million photographs to see if their children's photos are being used inappropriately online.

For safety and security reasons, all searches must be verified by either an authorized law enforcement officer or lawyer. This prevents online predators from abusing our system to further their cyberstalking.

www.Cyberbully.watch

DEDICATION

A special thanks to the educators who made an immeasurable impact on my life growing up; if it were not for you, I doubt I would be here today. I know I was one heck of a pain-in-the-butt, yet somehow you managed to not only put up with me but also to teach me a thing or two. Perseverance and self-reliance are probably the most important lessons you taught me.

Simple words cannot thank you enough.

(listed in alphabetical order)

Mrs. Anne Allen
Palm Harbor University High School

Mrs. Cindy Cruz
Palm Harbor University High School

Deputy Gina Engerer, School Resource Officer
Pinellas County Sheriff's Office/Palm Harbor Middle School

Coach Jim Felce
Palm Harbor University High School

Table of Contents

SECTION TWO: Educators

SECTION THREE: Parents

SECTION FOUR: Looking Forward

Foreword

I am a tech entrepreneur, which is a more elegant way of saying I am a *computer geek*. In school, I was harassed and humiliated for being a *nerd* by the *cool kids*. Those titles and many other less than polite names were yelled out to me daily throughout my years in school. As difficult as it was at times, I wore those titles like a badge of honor because I knew where I was going with my life. Yes, of course, there were some stumbling blocks along the way, but today I am far more successful than those students that made fun of me in school. Many of them are on their second or third marriage, or worse on their second or third "baby-daddy" or "baby-momma" and work dead end, low wage jobs. Their greatest excitement each week is cashing their check at the local check cashing joint then immediately blowing the money on smokes, beer, and lotto tickets. Whereas I own two successful tech companies, my own house, became certified as a Paramedic solely to volunteer for my community, have already published one book (this is the second), and my list of accomplishments goes on and on. I was stronger than them mentally; I knew it, and secretly, they knew it as well.

Yes, I know the above sounds extremely egotistical, and I must agree, but I felt it was essential to include it here as to communicate a very specific message:

We must teach our children to overcome the bullying of others
and how to use that anger as fuel to power their success.

Of course, that was then, and this is now. The ways bullies choose to inflict their pain today is far different than when you and I went to school. Things have changed, and methodologies on how to handle them must change as well. No longer can a student return to the safety of their home to be away from the bully. When I was bullied, I knew it only lasted the school day and possibly the walk or bike ride home, but once I was home and in my room, I was safe.

Today's bully follows the child right into their bedroom. Of course, I don't mean literally, but they do it virtually, through text messages and online forms of social media. Escaping this can be challenging for even the most mentally adept student. Throughout this book, I will cover exactly what cyberbullying is and how it differs from the schoolyard bullying of the past we knew. Then we will cover methodologies for educators, parents, lawmakers, and law enforcement to battle this rising foe online.

I will also discuss www.Cyberbully.watch, an online service I created to assist parents and educators in detecting and removing online cyberbullying and revenge pornography posts. The basic service is free for parents and educators; there are some premium features available as well. I invite you to check it out online at:

www.Cyberbully.watch

Introduction

The human race has come a long way; from the early days when humanity lived in caves and hunted animals in the wild to the days of the explorers who navigated around the globe in search of a habitable environment to live in, the human race has made significant inroads in virtually all aspects of life.

The internet, without doubt, has been one of the most significant and most impactful inventions of humanity. From banking to architecture, to medicine, to engineering, etc. the impact of the internet in elevating how humans live, relate, and communicate speaks for themselves.[1] Before its invention, mankind was already recording historical events, originally by song and storytelling than to the written word. For thousands of years, only the noble elites had the power to bring a story to a written form; this gave them the ability to control the narrative in ways that were most flattering to their image and detrimental to their enemies. With the introduction of the internet, now people of all socioeconomic classes have the power to express themselves freely and record events as they happen and from their viewpoint.

In the realms of communication, the internet has helped much in improving how messages and information are passed from one person

---

[1] Richards, J. (2005). Communication. North Mankato, MN: Chrysalis Education.

to another. It has bridged the gap and barriers to communication that existed due to the distance between the sender and the receiver in the communication chain. The world has become a global village due to the innovations in different communication channels brought about by the internet. The internet leveraged on the social and interpersonal nature of human beings in ensuring the flow of communication between friends, acquaintances, and strangers can be established and maintained if the need for that arises. This freedom to communicate and express the thoughts, feelings, and beliefs, while technically a byproduct of the 'invention' of the internet, I feel is far more impacting, both to the positive and negative upon humankind, than any other single event in history.

Social media is one of the contributions of the internet to human endeavor. Almost every member of civilized society has at least one social media account with many having multiple accounts across a multitude of platforms. Today platforms such as Facebook, Twitter, Instagram, WhatsApp, SecureTribe, and other various social media networks boast of millions and sometimes billions of subscribers all over the world.[2] This is a testament to the fact we are in the internet age, and social media has taken over the world. It is safe to say social media has grown so intertwined into our day-to-day lives. For some, it has had the unfortunate effect of completely replacing the need for face to face interaction. Users can now keep in touch with family and friends around the globe in real time as if they are physically in the same location at the same time.

Written texts, video, and voice call all of which have been adopted by many social media platforms have all played significant roles in sustaining communication among people. It is so well designed

---

[2] Meikle, G. (2016). Social media: Communication, sharing and visibility. London: Routledge.

activities such as teaching, chatting, talking, etc. can all be engaged in without the stress of arranging in-person meetings between the parties involved.[3]

Without a doubt, communication is the core of the human experience. All we do is a function of communication. Indeed, life is meaningless whenever communication cannot be attained with others. Social media, in spite of its numerous positive implications to man, is not without its flaws. One of these negative implications is cyberbullying. It is a serious issue that is sweeping across the world and just like a hurricane, it has caused inexplicable damage to people along its path. Families have been rendered childless, children have been rendered orphans, and so many other unfortunate events have occurred all because of this issue of cyberbullying.[4]

By the way, in the discourse of what cyberbullying is; two things are essential: the first is to define what cyberbullying truly is, and the second is to trace the roots and history of it. Cyberbullying can be described as the misuse of information and technology aimed towards harassing, intimidating, or harming other people emotionally, physically, or mentally; it can also be a combination of these things. It is usually enacted through the posting of negative comments, rumors, or photos of another person on the internet or social networking sites to embarrass or humiliate him/her in public, especially in front of their peers.[5]

Cyberbullying did not begin on its own; it is an offshoot of bullying. Bullying essentially refers to the repeated behavior of verbal and physical action from one person to another intended to cause

---

[3] Meikle, G. (2016). Social media: Communication, sharing and visibility. London: Routledge.

[4] Völlink, T., Dehue, F., & McGuckin, C. (2016). Cyberbullying: From theory to intervention. London: Routledge Taylor & Francis Group.

[5] Gerdes, L. I. (2012). Cyberbullying. Detroit: Greenhaven Press.

misery and emotional and/or physical pain upon the victim. By its very nature, bullying is more prominent among children and youths than among adults[6], yet it is not limited exclusively to children and does happen to adults more than we would expect. Notwithstanding, kids are more emotional than adults and tend to have less interpersonal skills; hence, they tend to be more volatile in their approach to issues and their management of tangible or intangible materials. This explains why the significant victims and perpetrators of bullying, cyberbullying, or any other form of bullying, are typically the younger generations. It is worthy of note to state at this juncture bullying takes place a lot within the school premises; of course, cyberbullying is perpetrated mostly outside the school premises and also does happen among adults.

Technology and the internet are the lifeblood of cyberbullying[7]. This is the primary reason why it is more widespread in countries with high usage of technologies and the internet. Cyberbullying is one very tricky problem to theorize and conceptualize. For instance, it is incredibly difficult to accurately determine the prevalence of cyberbullying among different age groups in society for two primary reasons:

1. Many instances of cyberbullying go unreported because either the victim feels it is not significant enough to warrant a criminal action to be instituted with the police, or the victim may be afraid they might not be believed or get justice.

---

[6] Völlink, T., Dehue, F., & McGuckin, C. (2016). Cyberbullying: From theory to intervention. London: Routledge Taylor & Francis Group.
[7] Völlink, T., Dehue, F., & McGuckin, C. (2016). Cyberbullying: From theory to intervention. London: Routledge Taylor & Francis Group.

2. Secondly, human behavior is dynamic, and what might be considered offensive by one may be regarded as usual chatter by another; hence the scope of what constitutes cyberbullying is incredibly difficult to decide; it differs from culture to culture and from individual to individual.[8]

3. Victims of cyberbullying may also be afraid of the repercussions he or she may face from the bully if help is sought out, but there are no true consequences to the bully.

Many victims of bullying due to the perceived helplessness of their state, rather than report the issue or take decisive steps to quell it, have continued to put up with it; while some have eventually been able to cope and adjust others have taken drastic steps. These include but are not limited to binge drinking, drug abuse, sexual promiscuity, and even suicide in some cases.

One undisputed characteristic of cyberbullying is it is different from the conventional forms of bullying which may involve physical assault as well as intimidation and aggression. Cyberbullying is fundamentally different from these types of bullying because it is often perpetrated through the use of electronic devices, and the audience is vast and almost limitless. This implies unlike school bullying, where the bully and the victim have to be present in a specific geographical location, cyberbullying is not bound by geography. An individual from another continent could be targeted by someone from the other side of the world as far as cyberbullying is concerned. Another critical factor about cyberbullying, which perhaps has added fuel to it and is responsible for its swift rise, is the fact it can be perpetrated

---

[8] Gerdes, L. I. (2012). Cyberbullying. Detroit: Greenhaven Press.

anonymously unlike the traditional bullying where the perpetrator can be easily described by their physical features, traced, arrested, and punished for their offense. Although most websites store cookies and caches of their users which could be used to track visitors to their sites, the fact remains it is difficult or at least requires more intelligence of technology, investigative time, and resources to capture the perpetrators of cyberbullying.

According to results from a longitudinal study conducted by Public Health England (PHE) and released in 2017, based upon consultation and interview with teenagers mostly aged between 11 and 15 years, 17.9% of those surveyed admitted to being cyberbullied in the two months preceding their meeting with the PHE. This merely confirms the suspicion regarding the wide prevalence and occurrence of this criminal act in the world today. The unrestricted availability of internet-enabled gadgets has seemingly encouraged this activity so bullies can specifically target other internet users with all manner of vile and despicable insults and abuse hurled at them unashamedly, due to their perceived anonymity and sense of security the internet tends to provide.

Cyber-stalking is one of the most commonly propagated forms of cyberbullying. It refers to the scenarios where stalkers deliberately wait for their target to upload or post so they can then upload vile and/or threatening messages towards or to their target. A report from Anti-bullying Alliance UK theorizes girls are more likely to be both the victim and the perpetrator of cyberbully than boys. In other words, there is a gender disparity when it comes to the discourse about cyberbullying. This trend might not be unconnected with the fact girls tend to be more body conscious and potentially envious of one another than boys. With regards to this trend, girls tend to be cyberbullied through name-calling and social exclusion. Another reason why girls are likely to be victims of cyberbullying than boys is the fact they are more interactive on social media sites than boys. Generally, an observation of the comments in a regular entertainment blog on social media sites such as Facebook, Twitter, and Instagram is likely to reveal more female 'commenters' than males. Also, it must be noted when it comes to uploading pictures on the internet, the females come out the undisputed winner. All of these factors are weighty in the discourse on why females face more cyberbullying than their male counterparts.

Cyberbullying just as it can be more prevalent with one gender more than the other also tends to increase with age. Indeed, the seeds of bullying have been sown in children from a very young age tend to grow and continue to propagate with time. It is often said that time heals all wounds, but one other thing about time is it emphasizes compound human character. A lousy character developed from childhood is not likely to decrease but rather to widen with time. Physical bullying which is common among school-aged children tends to reduce with age mainly due to the fear of discipline and humiliation by the school authorities if discovered, or for fear of the victim seeking redress with the law enforcement agencies. However, cyberbullying tends to rise with age. It feeds on the natural human inclination to seek power and domination over one another. Naturally, human society would be lawless if there were no rules and punishment for behavior. It is the threat of sanctions that often puts people in check. Because the risk of penalty for cyberbullying is lower compared to other forms of bullying, the behavior, therefore, tends to increase even with age. Thus, the bullies who grew up with the attitude of bullying others then mature and raise kids who observe the bullying attitudes of their parents and begin to unconsciously appropriate these behaviors innocently in their dealings with their colleagues in the playgroup or at school; thus continues the propagation of bullying in the society.

As discussed earlier, it is a typical human trait to dominate each other. This is the thirst to have power and control over another. This is why bullies are typically insecure people who are envious of something the others have; this could range from tangible to intangible such as happiness, status, money, influence, car, money or even power. Bullying is majorly a manifestation of jealousy for something seen in others but lacking within themselves. This is precisely why celebrities are always victims of bullies who feel they should have an opinion on how others should live their lives and conduct themselves. They attempt to control the lives of others by sowing the seeds of misery and despair into them so they can feel better about themselves.

I am sure this is not the first book you have read about schoolyard bullying; I too have read many of them. Each left me with the same problem; they were full of "content" but completely lacking in actionable ideas. Throughout this book, I will attempt to fill in the pieces where, I feel, the other literature fails.

SECTION ONE

History of Schoolyard Bullying

As I am sure you will agree with me the concept of schoolyard bullying is not new and has most likely existed since the beginning of humankind. It is a phenomenon that has affected the entire human society, and up until this point, bullying has a not too good history.

Ever since the very first schoolyard, there has been schoolyard bullying. The evolution of formal learning resulted in the creation of schools wherein children were gathered to be taught different subjects by seasoned teachers. As the schoolchildren learn valuable lessons and skills from their teachers, they also brought their different personalities to intermingle with other children. While some children with quiet and timid personalities mingled through peaceful means, some others decided to express their frustrations through bullying their schoolmates.

As far back as the 1530s, 'bullying' became a regularly used word in society. In its purest form, it connoted the relationship between two individuals, a bully who intimidates and a victim who is receptive to the intimidation. In many ways back then, and now, the bully always abused the victim through physical, verbal, and other abuse. As always, the bully aims to get superiority over the victims. The occurrence of a bully inflicting harm on another victim to improve his perceived self worth and social status among his peers has always been present.

School is a big part of childhood and the upbringing of every child. Hence, unchecked bullying is a severe external factor that not only could cause significant damage to the mindset of the child, it could corrupt their perception of relationships, and could potentially set the stage for long-lasting damage which could extend beyond childhood and growing onward to puberty adulthood.

Bullying is a notoriously difficult concept to describe, because it is not just restricted to physical exertion alone, but it also includes psychological torment which in most instances is difficult to conceptualize. Victims of bullying may find it difficult to prove and seek justice from the proper authorities, especially when the nature of the bullying involved is psychological rather than physical. Except for the activities of children that are monitored throughout the school hours with their verbal expressions and body language being observed in real time, it would be impossible to decisively stem the tide of the presence of bullying in the school premises.

While most as educators and parents wish to have the ability to wave a magic wand and remove the pain from bullying hesitation must be used before trying to step in and fix all problems so the child has the opportunity to problem solve on their own. Good, bad, or indifferent, interacting with bullies is a necessary part of growing up and learning valuable interpersonal skills that the youth will use into adulthood and throughout the rest of their life.

Just as important to know what bullying is, it must be understood what bullying isn't. Not all acts of unkindness among youth should be called bullying, and out of the situations that are apparent bullying, very few actually, require direct and immediate adult intervention. Remember by experiencing these painful situations, children learn and grow. It is a sad fact, but there are jerks in this world, and no level of coddling a child will change that fact. A child must be taught how to handle the emotional aspects of life when mean people do unkind things.

Cyberbullying:
The 21st Century School Yard

The concept of bullying is almost as old as humanity itself. Anywhere humans exist, the tendency to seek dominion over one another is a given. Perhaps it is not just restricted to humans; animals exhibit traits of dominance over one another. Anywhere there is a consistent and regular gathering of people, it is typical for a few members of the population to show domineering traits over another; this is why schools have been such a natural breeding ground for bullying for such a long time.

Three characteristics that are generally agreed upon as present in all cases of bullying[9]:

1. *Power imbalance:* The child who is the bully wields greater power--usually as a result of a high social status

2. *Repeated occurrence:* Bullying happens repeatedly--it's not a one-time encounter, even if a cruel one-time encounter occurs

3. *Intentionality:* Bullying is not an accident or an incident misinterpreted as an act of cruelty. Bullying is a dysfunctional relationship between two children. These children may or may not "know" each other in the traditional sense, but they do interact repeatedly.[10]

Being confined in a single location consistently during the day is bound to bring out the real personality of that person. This is why one of the best institutions to observe human behavior in its natural form is the school. Children begin to show their dominant and subjective sides based on their evaluation of others around them. This perhaps is the reason why the school is the place with the highest power play as individuals struggle within themselves to gain powers over another in a way that mimics the political arena.

In previous generations, bullying took place on the actual playground, hallways, classrooms, and other parts of the school and usually involved a student that was physically larger, relatively weak academically, and not particularly admired by other kids in the

---

[9] D. Olweus, *Aggression in the Schools: Bullies and Whipping Boys* (Oxford, England: Hemisphere, 1978), http://psycnet.apa.org/psycinfo/1979-32242-000
[10] Elizabeth Kandel Englander, *Bullying and Cyberbullying: What every educator needs to know*, 2013. p 15

school.[11] A bully would target a student he or she thought was vulnerable and harass them. Sometimes it would be the old stealing the milk money or verbal threats like, *"meet me behind the gym after class, and I'm gonna beat you."*

Although bullying has been around for quite a while, the advent of the internet has only gone ahead to amplify bullying by creating a sub-division of it, which is known as cyberbullying. No longer is the bully standing directly in front of their victim. Now, the bully can hide behind the anonymity of a pseudonym, making it challenging to identify the actual culprit.

In an effort to protect children, today's youth are far more supervised during the school day than previous generations. This has had the unintended effect of causing *"normalization of bullying behaviors by requiring bullies to adopt methods that can be used in more public areas,"*[12] such as the abuse of technology to bully their victims.

Nowadays, it is a rarity to come across a child who has not been affected in some way by bullying in recent times. According to the Pediatric Academic Societies in their general meeting held 5th of May, 2013 in Washington DC:

> *Step into a class of 30 high school students and look around, five of them have been victims of electronic bullying in the past year.* [13]

---

[11] D. Olweus, *Aggression in the Schools: Bullies and Whipping Boys* (Oxford, England: Hemisphere, 1978), http://psycnet.apa.org/psycinfo/1979-32242-000

[12] Elizabeth Kandel Englander, *Bullying and Cyberbullying: What every educator needs to know*, 2013. p 17

[13] Science Daily, American Academy of Pediatrics, May 5, 2013, "*Cyberbullying rampant among high school students:*" https://www.sciencedaily.com/releases/2013/05/130505073738.htm

Psychologically, when a behavior is not punished, it is rewarded. The lack of stringent measures to tackle bullying in school has led to a steady rise in bullying everywhere in the world today. Bullies who started in the school having graduated from schools into a higher school level or into the workplace and continue to exhibit and practice their bullying unrestrained, therefore, making the society less and less healthy by the day. A cursory look towards major governmental agencies and public office holders easily reflect this trend of bullies now occupying positions of the authority having graduated from school and continued to master and hone their art everywhere they find themselves unashamedly.

> *"Psychologically contemptuous, rue behaviors are called gateway behaviors, since they are used as beginning or low-level, low-risk ways of asserting power or expression contempt."[14]*

Without proper intervention, these gateway behaviors can increase in frequency and escalate in severity.[15] Research shows gateway behaviors are used substantially more often than other, more apparent types of bullying behaviors. In 2012, only 6% of respondents reported being victims of physical bullying while in high school, but 34% reported being victims of distressing rumors or lies.[16]

It is evident the issue with cyberbullying is connected to the usage of the internet. Hence, it is apparent the usability of the internet is the major problem more than the children themselves. Yes, it is true multiple factors combine to contribute to bullying ideation in children, yet there seems reasonable evidence to suggest early exposure to the

---

[14] Elizabeth Kandel Englander, *Bullying and Cyberbullying: What every educator needs to know*, 2013. p 17

[15] U.S. Department of Education, *Bully: Per Abuse in Schools*, LD Online, 1998, http://www.ldonline.org/article/6171

[16] E. Englander, *Cyberbullying - New Research and Findings*, presented at the 2012 National Cyber Crime Conference, Norwood, Massachusetts, 2012.

technological gadgets and the internet has made the issue more complicated than it naturally ought to be. The internet promotes anonymity, and when this is in place, many unsocial and negative traits inherent in human beings begin to come out and manifest naturally.

Children must be educated on their powers and abilities to resist being bullied either by their teachers, by their colleagues, and by their parents. Conferences can be organized to motivate them on the need to believe in themselves, ignore the bullies, not fight back, and report to the authorities if they are bullied again. Bullying is not a one and for all event; it tends to be repeated due to the bully seeking to stamp his authority on his victim and build a fear factor around himself. The fight to reclaim the integrity of the school system back must begin from here. It will no doubt be an arduous and tasking one, but it will be one where the reward outweighs the sacrifices involved.

Children are highly impressionable, and a lot must be done to protect and shield them from exposure to antisocial behaviors either at home or at school. Parents must be orientated on acts that reasonably constitute bullying so they can adjust their conduct at home and everywhere accordingly. Parents are first of all role models for their children; hence, they must play their role well as role models and ensure they only replicate acts that are wholesome and loving before their children. The upbringing of children is a joint venture between teacher and parents; hence, teachers should work with school authorities to promote healthy communication and relationship between students at all times, and where a child consistently exhibits bullying tendencies toward his peers, the parents must be contacted and urged to address the issue with their child appropriately.

The school may recommend and advise parents on the best approach to handling the issue. It is imperative that teachers and parents be made aware of the severity of bullying on the mental and emotional development of children. It is an act that can rob the society of brilliant inventions and innovations can advance the course of humanity and make life easier and more pleasant. Worse of all, bullying is an act that can bring about suicidal thoughts and ideation that can rob families of their precious children. This is why schoolyard bullying is an activity that must be tackled headlong.

Notwithstanding, it is important to repeat and elaborate on the point made in the previous section that not all activities of unkindness warrant direct intervention from adults. As painful as it may be to watch, children must learn tactics to handle meanness from others, and adults should only intervene when it is necessary. It is the responsibility of adults to know when intervention in a situation to prevent or at least reduce the damage done to another child is required. Only through educational programs of all parties involved, educators, parents, and children, both those could be victims and those could be perpetrators, can we hope to make a positive impact.

This education starts with reducing the overuse of the words bully and victim.

OVERUSE OF THE TERMS "BULLY" AND "VICTIM"

I, the author, feel we must take a moment and discuss how terms like "bully" and "victim" are overused, and how this overuse of the words is harmful to real victims of bullying.

If you rank of popular words in America today, one word that is bound to be prominent in the result is the word "bully." Without any doubt, bullying is an activity that deserves every attention that is being paid to it around the world, and perhaps even more attention is needed. However, there is a somewhat strange aura about the bully in schools, workplaces, and society at large; there seems to be a misconception of what qualifies as bullying. Anytime the word is mentioned, the mood automatically shifts from casual to serious because the gravity of the consequences that accompany the act is endless.

It is clear from times past, a lot has been done to stem the tide of bullying in human society and yet if you watch the 24-hour news channels or read a news article online, everyone is seemingly a victim of bullying. It does not matter if the report is about a divorce case in court with one of the two parties labeling the other party as a bully or for a student to name his classmate as a bully, or for the President to be called a bully just because he does not follow the same political ideology of another.

The use of the word is also common in the workplace as subordinates and superiors often slam the word on any individual or character they often disagree with. It is impossible to disagree with another without you being labeled a bully.

The word "bully" is so commonly used in the society today the average person already believes they know exactly what the word means, and they do not bother to read a dictionary to find its actual definition, Merriam Webster Dictionary[17] defines a *bully* as:

> *a blustering, browbeating person especially : one who*
> *is habitually cruel, insulting, or threatening to others*
> *who are weaker, smaller, or in some way vulnerable*

The key is *habitually* cruel to others. It also goes on to define a bully as a tormenter who has an imbalance of power and uses this behavior

---

[17] Merriam Webster Dictionary Online, definition of *bully* https://www.merriam-webster.com/dictionary/bully

towards others on a constant basis. It is imperative the true meaning of a word be properly understood before being applied and used; otherwise, it may lead to a problem, especially with developing laws to tackle issues. After all, the problem has to be fully understood before help can be proposed. In the definition above, some key factors are essential or necessary for a person's actions to be aptly termed as "bullying."

According to the definition above, among other things, a bully must habitually cruel, i.e. have a track record of cruelty in his dealings with others around him. The bully must also be a tormenter, i.e. he must be an individual that thrives and derives joy from seeing others in pain and anguish. He or she must also have an inordinate appetite for power and dominion, so he wants to impose his opinions and ideas on others forcefully and aggressively on a regular basis. Based on these clarifications, a bully must be consistently aggressive towards his victims.

Bringing this definition back to the schoolyard or even to online social media based cyberbullying, the bully must be relentless and consistent in the torment of their victim(s). An isolated instance with the passing of a comment like "she is fat" or "look at those zits, dork" is an example of being a jerk, not a bully. Of course, I am not saying those comments should be made or as educators and parents to ignore the comments. Being a jerk is not acceptable, and it must be taught to the youth those comments are not socially acceptable. I am saying these examples, which account for many cases of bullying, do not rise to the level of victimization and calling them such only diminishes the words.

"So who cares?" is what you are probably thinking, right? What is the harm in calling a simple schoolyard jerk a bully and the target of his or her meanness a victim? The harm is when you lump these cases together into the same grouping with instances of real torment by true bullies. More specifically, everyone will become desensitized to the term bully; when a youth wishes to report an actual instance of bullying to adults, it can be too easily dismissed as "kids will be kids." If everyone is a victim, then nobody is.

Another critical reason to distinguish between name calling and fights compared to actual cases of bullying is in most cases of kids getting into fights, verbal or even physical, it is a two-way street. Whereas, bullying is one way with the target of victimization innocent of any wrongdoing.

Children are not stupid, and in some ways, they are more cunning than adults give them credit. Kids know if they run to an adult and say, "he is being a bully and picking on me," the adult will storm over to the bully and stop the action. This will happen even if, unbeknown to the adult, both children were equal in their unkindness towards each other. In these cases, which account for many, who is the victim? Was it the child that ran to the adult or the purported bully? I feel the alleged bully was the victim as he or she will undoubtedly receive punishment; whereas the other kid that reported the alleged act was most likely just as guilty. Do not blindly allow a child to assume the role of a victim without investigation.

Only by separating the occasional name calling and simple fights in the schoolyard from constant tormenting of another can we ever help to remedy the situation. Of course, just as I stated above, schoolyard fights and name calling should still be addressed at the administrative level with adequate punishment for all parties guilty, it should not be considered or called bullying.

Now that what bullying is not has been discussed let's rummage into what it actually is; this will help expose the glaring overuse of the term in our society today. Bullying can be broken down into four main groups; physical, verbal, social, and material:

- Bullying can be physical when it involves acts such as tripping, pushing intentionally, hitting, or striking a person.

- It can be verbal when it involves the use of insulting words to threaten, mock, and ridicule another person. Verbal bullying can also include the use of hostile remarks such as sexist or racist remarks or the use of stereotypic statements that discriminate against or unjustly amplify the physical defects or characteristics of a person. Bullying can be termed as social bullying when it involves consciously propagating lies and rumors about someone to smear their image and deplete their worth in society.

- Social bullying also involves such acts and behaviors that are targeted at isolating and excluding an individual from group activity in a bid to humiliate them.

- Material bullying, just as the name suggests, include the deliberate destruction and vandalism of goods or property belonging to someone else. It can also involve forcefully or falsely taking something belonging to someone without their prior consent, i.e., taking a kid's lunch money or another item with or without value.

On the other hand, we must also itemize and discuss acts that do not constitute bullying. Based on the dynamic nature of human behavior, it is quite easy to categorize any unwanted or diversionary behavior from someone as bullying even when it is not.

EXPRESSING A DIFFERENCE IN OPINION IS NOT BULLYING:

Regardless of whatever the situation or circumstance at play, a person has the right to disagree with another person; however, consistently such disagreement has occurred in other conversations. A person has a right to his opinion and must be able to express such without bias or being labeled as a bully. In a lot of the instances where the allegations of bullying have been leveled, some are likely to be premised on a constant disagreement between two or more persons.

Disagreement is a regular occurrence in human societies. This is due to a lot of reasons such as differences in personality, differences in socioeconomic status, differences in gender, and indeed differences in intelligence and cognition. Whenever disagreements occur, rather than it be perceived as a negative happening, it should be welcomed and examined because differences in opinion can help throw in different ideas that can bring about significant improvements and changes.

DISLIKE OF A PERSON'S CHARACTER IS NOT BULLYING:

Without any doubt, it is best we love everyone around us. It is better for our health and mental development. Hating or disliking someone is an unnecessary burden on the mind. No matter how nice of fantasy this is, human nature is not that kind. Some people are just unpleasant to be around, and you are under no obligation in a free society to like everyone around you. So far as you do not go out of your way to harass, harm, or intimidate them, then it is not necessarily wrong to dislike someone. This cannot be termed as bullying.

EXPRESSION OF UNPLEASANT THOUGHTS OR FEELINGS REGARDING OTHERS IS NOT BULLYING:

In most Westernized democracies around the world, the freedom of expression is still a fundamental human right for every citizen, and in the U.S. this constitutional provision no doubt confers on individuals the right and privilege to express their minds about issues especially on those about them and others.

In the discussion about bullying, it must be noted regular acts of disagreements and deference, however consistent they are, are not enough to qualify as bullying. Alternatively, repressed thoughts can lead to mental and emotional issues; it is suitable for individuals to express themselves whenever the need arises. What is necessary, however, is these acts of self-expression be done civilly without insult. For instance, a teacher yelling at an unruly student in class does not qualify as bullying. Likewise, a parent reprimanding her son for being rude is not bullying.

IGNORING OTHERS IS NOT AN ACT OF BULLYING:

You have a right to ignore anyone you have reservations about. It is essential children understand not everyone around them may like them, and this should not necessarily be perceived as bullying. Just because a classmate does not want to sit with another student at lunch does not mean they are a bully.

Everyone has a right to choose their associations and the way they behave and respond to others around them. It is invasive and unlawful to impose yourself on others. Indeed, quite ironically, it will amount to bullying for you to expect everyone to accept you and be cordial towards you.

THE OVERUSE OF THESE TERMS CAUSES CONFUSION

"The scope and effect of bullying are underestimated."[18]
"Bullying is more common than previously thought."[19]
"The level of playground bullying is being exaggerated"[20]
"online survey showed 91% of respondents claimed they were bullied."[21]
"6% of students were bullied in the last year."[22]

I could go on for pages citing quote after quote that contradict each other. Some states show a whopping 91% of students claimed to be bullied, and other states only 6%. Obviously, both statistics cannot be accurate.

One might wonder as to how this can be true? If the facts prove bullying is getting worse, then shouldn't all the studies and quoted citations represent a consensus of the information? The problem, I feel, is in how bullying is defined. As we have already discussed in this chapter, the terms *bully* and *victim* get tossed around so often and in cases where they are not applicable that the original meaning of those words is lost.

---

[18] http://www.safeandcaringschools.com
[19] http://www.ashleypsychology.com
[20] http://www.theneweditor.com
[21] StageOfLife.com 2011 self reported online poll
[22] 2009 National Crime Victimization Survey

Why do Children Bully?

The use of social media is very prevalent among school-aged children all over the world today. We all know teenagers use social media, but some may not realize youths as young as eight or nine are using these platforms as well. Technically some laws prevent or at least restrict online usage for minors under the age of 14 in the United States, but kids easily bypass these age restrictions by lying about their age.

These pre-teens are still undergoing the stages of physical and emotional growth. One of the physical and emotional changes that come with puberty is the development of social and interpersonal skills.

This is why school-aged children are more fixated with social interaction than adults. The consistent communication between children in school and on the internet plays a significant role in their concept of personal identity. They often begin to compare themselves with others around them, thereby evaluating themselves through the eyes of others, and this may pose a severe problem in it can lead to inferiority or superiority complex in children.

Without a doubt, a lot has been written and said about the prevalence of cyberbullying in the world today and its effect on the social, physical, and emotional well-being of its victims. In postulating a wholesome discussion of the subject, there is an inherent need to beam the searchlight on the primary reasons why bullying has continued to flourish.

Without a doubt, bullying is antithetical to the society's well being as it tends to lead towards a host of unhealthy consequences in society such as drugs abuse, poor or underwhelming academic performance, truancy, suicide, depression, and other unfavorable outcomes. Bullying may seem a significant evil that has eaten deep into the fabric of the society, but by examining its root causes, possible routes towards its resolution can thus be charted. There are many reasons why children bully each other, and they are going to be examined simultaneously in the following succeeding paragraphs.

Environmental factors are one of the most fundamental elements of why children bully. The environment is a significant precursor of human behavior because somehow, we are likely to reflect the norms and culture of the situation where we are raised. Hence a child grew in a home where one or both parents bully one another openly utilizing verbal and physical assault; it is most likely such a child will likely mirror the characters of the parents. Childhood is a very significant period of life because it is the stage of life that embodies gullibility than any other stage. Children are highly impressionable; they learn a lot by observing the actions of their parents toward each other as well as towards neighbors, and they innocently and unconsciously reproduce these characters in themselves.

There is another angle that must be considered in the way environmental factors influence bullying tendencies in children, and it is parenting style. Children raised by permissive parents are likely to become bullies. This is of course not an inevitable consequence because there might be children raised by permissive parents who still turned out to be responsible and well-behaved students, but the likelihood exists children raised by permissive parents tend to gravitate towards bullying naturally. A 2012 study on bullying posted in the *Journal of Cybertherapy and Rehabilitation* speculated the lazy approach to parenting rewards bullying traits in children. The norm of behavior is desirable behaviors should be rewarded and unhelpful behaviors should be punished. This ought to be the standard for raising children; when there is no threat of sanction by parents or caregivers, children tend to become unruly and oppressive towards one another.

Peer pressure is another reason why children are likely to bully one another. Just like every other age group, children mingle with one another and make friends easily. Depending on the personalities and behavioral disposition of the company children keep around themselves, they are likely to take on their behaviors in a bid to conform and blend.

According to Abraham Maslow's hierarchy of needs[23], the need for belongingness is an inherent human need, and this is because

---

[23] Maslow's hierarchy of needs, via Wikipedia
https://en.wikipedia.org/wiki/Maslow%27s_hierarchy_of_needs

belonging to a group is one of the ways humans derive happiness. Living life alone is not an appealing prospect; this is the reason why humans always seek to identify with different groups, especially those they feel might protect their interests. Every human being belongs to some groups at any point in time. The family is the first group every human being consciously or unconsciously belongs. Regardless of the circumstances of birth, every child has a father and a mother, and the child is likely to be enrolled in a school at some point which will be composed of a group of people.

Whatever group we belong, there is a perceived reward or benefit for being a member of such a group; this is what keeps any group enticing and appealing for others to want to join; when others join, they want to do everything to maintain their membership of the group, and if this involves bullying then so be it. Children previously well-behaved might begin to join their mates in bullying others for fear of being ostracized from their group or even being degraded and bullied in return for their inability to join their mates in bullying.

Prejudice and stereotype is another cause of bullying among school children. We all have friends or at least have some people we admire. In this case, children always feel the need to form cliques among themselves. In an average classroom today, the class is usually divided by the various students. Everyone has their friends who they confide and relate. Each group of friends sees themselves as better than the other, and if this rivalry is left to thrive, it can become unhealthy, outgrowing the boundary of the classroom and the schoolyard into the pages of social media.

Furthermore, when we talk about prejudice as a factor promoting bullying in schools, it means children with disabilities are likely to be more at the receiving end of bullying by fellow students making a jest of their looks or disabilities. This could be disheartening and discouraging for such children who may feel inadequate as compared to their colleagues, they may, as a result, develop an inferiority complex. They may want to quit school or become aloof due to their feeling of inadequacy to schooling activities. Unfortunately, most have no choice other than to complete schooling. Religious beliefs are also influential factors promoting stereotypes in children. Children practicing religions which are in the minority in an environment may be laughed at or teased; this occurs more frequently when another child has only heard negative thoughts about this religion from the adults that surround them. Race and sexual orientation are also a hot button that may increase the propensity to indulge in bullying. It is safe to say some form of prejudice is always somewhere at the root cause of bullying, either online or offline.

The desire for attention is another reason why children bully. Every human being wants to be loved, cared for, and cherished by others. This need is relevant to all age groups, including children. At close examination, it is apparent bullying is often evidence of a character flaw among children. Children who feel unloved and unappreciated may seek attention by bullying others.

Bullies, in many instances, also lack good communication skills. Their lack of excellent communication skills might lead to loneliness due to difficulty in making friends, hence their resolve to take drastic action to mitigate the trend. They may begin innocently by trying to create communication with others, but if they are refused, they might become frustrated and feel the right thing to do is to force themselves on others. Rather than warm their way into the hearts of others, they tend to push their way into it. This apparent deficiency in communication skills is why some bullies live in denial of the wickedness and mischief posed by their actions. They feel they are not necessarily wrong as they were merely trying to make friends even though they were forcing themselves on others, which is outrightly against the established norms of behavior in any civilized culture. Some of them might not necessarily recognize verbal assault as bullying, even when it is.

One of the most troubling and disconcerting thoughts posed by bullying is it might be an indication of sadism. Perhaps this is why parents, school authorities, and government agencies in charge of education needs to do more. Childhood is the foundation of life. It is a stage where many behavioral dispositions are formed and developed throughout the cause of life. As troubling as it may seem, some people derive pleasure from seeing others writhing in pain and anguish. They may feel their environment is dull and there is a need for an injection of excitement to liven things up, and as a result of this, they resort to intimidating and harassing others to make themselves feel happy at all costs. These individuals often become sociopaths and psychopaths later in life.

A child who is already a bully if left unpunished may propagate that behavior until it eventually gets so pronounced and becomes a problem to the broader society. As children get fortified in the art of bullying, they may resort to seeking creative methods to express their evil actions towards their victims, especially if they discover their victims are now beginning to react instead of ignoring them. Alternatively, they may get bored by their former methods and begin to develop newer ways of getting across to their victims more decisively and severely. This resolve to innovating and curating new ways begins to stifle their empathetic feelings while also watering their cruel, and inhumane side which might manifest in their conduct, and behavior towards others in the society. Behavior is transient, what started as a little concern was waived off by the parents and teachers of the child may be what the greater community may pay dearly for in the coming future.

Among the reasons why children bully, the quest for power is a big factor. Just as I postulated earlier, humans naturally seek to dominate one another. Children with such strong appeal for power will likely develop narcissistic traits which would make them have condescending views of each other and attempt to relate with others around them strictly based on their terms which in this case turns out to be oppressive of the other party. Children with a bigger body build will likely seek to impose themselves upon others based on their perception of their physically intimidating frame.

In other ways, children with slightly better socioeconomic status might want to intimidate other students with more modest means. However, this fact is not a given as children from poorer backgrounds may also turn out to be bullies depending on the interplay of other factors, some of which have been discussed above. Their insecurity drives them to feel threatened, and hence, they resort to aggression rather than self-development and building their self-confidence in addressing the issue.

Top Forms of Cyberbullying

Because the internet is continually changing, users will find unique ways to abuse the social media tools provided to them to harm and bully others. Here we will cover a few of the most common forms of cyberbullying, but first let's distinguish between the intentional infliction of harm to another from unintentional harassment, or simply put 'being annoying.'

While technically harassment, some forms of communications, even if repetitive and unwanted, are not meant to be harmful to their recipient and any harm done is entirely unintentional. People do not necessarily have to have malice in their intent to harass somebody. For instance, when a boy keeps on sending unwanted messages to a girl every hour of the day it can be considered as harassment. If his intentions are not to cause harm, he does not have the interpersonal skills to know how to interact with a girl, then this is more of a case where clear communication from the young lady can go a long way to clear up the confusion. If after a definite *"no thank you, please do not contact me."* message does not stop the unwanted messages, then we move into true harassment and cyberbullying.

FLAMING

Flaming involves the repeated exchange of words between individuals online. Flaming in cyberbullying is not different from the normal flaming we experience every day. Imagine you are walking home and you met an old friend who you have some unpleasant history with. He is with three of his friends, but you are alone. All of a sudden, he calls you an insulting name and you curse back. Then his friends starts by saying things like; *'Are you going to let him disrespect you like that?'* In this scenario, his friends are flaming him. But the real flaming started when the two of you started exchanging words.

This is the same thing on the cyberspace; flame wars are frequent in public social media platforms like Twitter, Facebook, and other major forums. It draws in many people who are most likely going to take sides. This can lead to severe cyberbullying if not kneaded from the bud, it will escalate even beyond cyberspace.

DENIGRATION

This is a form of cyberbullying which involves the attempts of damaging one's reputation by circulating information that either shouldn't be shared or knowledge that is rooted in gossip and rumors. In most cases, denigration is beyond just social media and instant messaging platforms. Some bullies can go to the extent of using blogs, discussion groups, and online polls to denigrate their victims. One specific thing about this type of bullying is most young people who are victims do not like talking about it. This is because it is what it is; it is an attack on their image and self-esteem.

EXCLUSION

Before now, exclusion used to be in situations where young people are not invited to parties or hangouts. But these days, it has become easier to gather a bunch of friends in virtual spaces for activities like online group meetings, forums, parties, and even multi-player games. Although this action may appear to have less direct impacts on the victims, it is a form of cyberbullying and may become worse, especially if it goes on for a very long time. Sometimes members of these virtual groups tend to gang up against the person that is being excluded, and this may lead to other forms of cyberbullying.

Researches have shown victims of exclusion cyberbullying mostly suffer from low self-esteem; they tend to go in search for other groups that will accept them, and this may either result in another form of exclusion or to revenge. For instance, in a quest to have a sense of belonging, a victim of exclusion may look for another group to join, and in doing so, the said victim might be looking for the perfect way to carry out revenge on the people that had excluded him earlier.

OUTING

Friends often share secrets that they promise to keep. However, when friends fight, it's easy to break the promise and tell everyone the secret. The outing of a person is a cyberbullying form which is used by cyberbullies to "share" publicly private information without the consent of the victim to hurt them. It is different from denigration in the sense it is directed at harming the victim, not necessarily denting the person's image.[24]

CYBERSTALKING

Cyberstalking is a kind of harassment. However, harassing victims is not necessary. Victims typically receive electronic messages from cyberbullies that threaten and despise them. Such messages are highly intimidating and tend to give victims deep fear. Victims often begin to believe "the bully can go offline and harm them physically," which can also cause them to be overly suspicious of their environment. Cyberstalking in most countries is considered as a cybercrime, mostly for the number of deaths in young people that have in one way or the other been tied to it. In a bid to tackle cyberstalking, a lot of developed countries have established laws, but even at that, it is still rampant.

HAPPY SLAPPING

Happy Slapping is a new kind of cyberbullying stemmed forth from the evolution of internet-enabled mobile devices. It incorporates the rapid growth in online video contents and traditional bullying. Unlike most of the forms discussed so far, this is the one that cannot be defined just by looking at the words. However, if you are wondering what precisely happy slapping means, it is when a target child or suspect is attacked or embarrassed physically, and in the course of doing this, it is recorded with a mobile device. The images or video are recorded in this event will then be posted for public consumption

---

[24] Outing/Trickery. (n.d.). Retrieved from
https://cyberbullyingisevil.weebly.com/outingtrickery.html

online. Video blogging sites like Instagram and YouTube are some of the favorite platforms for bullies to share happy slapping.[25]

TEXT WARS AND TEXT ATTACKS

Text Wars and Text Attacks are cyberbullying tactics perpetrated by sending hundreds of emails or text messages by the cyberbully and a group of his/her accomplices. It is usually a form of gang up aimed at frustrating and putting fear in their victim's mind.

RUMOR SPREADING

Rumors are uncontrolled streams of information people circulate to make sense of unclear situations or address a possible threat.[26] Rumors deal with local problems or situations. They are somewhat like news; however, while news comes with definite proof, rumors don't. Instead, they are collective efforts aimed at building a make-believe story or to manage threats. Physical or psychological risks may arise during the cause of the whole process, which is precisely where rumor spreading, as regards to bullying, comes to play.

The subject of rumor spreading is one in which social psychologists have been interested in since the 1920s. It is interesting to know there are mathematical formulas and models geared towards breaking down what rumor spreading is all about. Generally, it has been discovered that rumor spreading is categorized into three categories:

- The first is *Dread* rumors, which generally conveys fear about a negative event.

---

[25] What is 'happy slapping'? - BBC Newsround. (2011, June 24). Retrieved from https://www.bbc.co.uk/newsround/amp/13905969

[26] Bordia, P., & DiFonzo, N. (2002). When social psychology became less social: Prasad and the history of rumor research. Asian Journal of Social Psychology, 5, 49-61.

- *Wish* rumors which are related to having the desired outcome of a situation.

- Finally, there are *Wedge-driving* rumors which are aimed at causing a division within a group[27].

Out of these three categories, bullies have frequently used dread rumors and wedge-driving rumors. For example, a bully can target a victim by spreading wedge-driving type of rumor to separate the victim from friends. This, of course, may lead to loneliness and depression, especially if the victim is not cleared of the rumors.[28]

When there is a negative rumor the morale of any grouping of people will be reduced along with a noticeable drop in trust. Wedge-driving rumors help form or strengthen prejudicial attitudes. Generally, it has been discovered rumors play significant roles in sparking riots when there are ethnic or racial tensions already. Rumors have also been found to alter the stock market prices as well as inducing critical health issues such as heart problems, etc. Interestingly, rumors do not have to be believed to have such devastating effects.[29] For example, hamburger sales at McDonald's took a temporary hit because of a false rumor that McDonald's burgers contained worm-meat; this happened even though most people actually disbelieved the rumor.[30]

The occurrence of rumor spreading is one that continues to remain devastating within every situation as the individuals being desecrated

[27] Allport, G. W., & Postman, L. J. (1947). The psychology of rumor. New York: Holt, Rinehart & Winston.

[28] Allport, G. W., & Postman, L. J. (1947). The psychology of rumor. New York: Holt, Rinehart & Winston.

[29] DiFonzo, N., & Bordia, P. (2007). Rumor psychology: Social & organizational approaches. Washington, DC: American Psychological Association.

[30] Saul, H. (2014, October 16). McDonald's answers pink slime and worm meat rumours by inviting. https://www.independent.co.uk/life-style/food-and-drink/mcdonald-s-answers-pink-slime-and-worm-meat-rumours-by-inviting-cameras-into-burger-factory-9793468.html

usually encounters many painful attacks to their self-esteem and mental state of mind. To display how much rumor spreading can be so devastating, some brilliant filmmakers within the Hollywood industry have devoted resources into engaging in the production of films aimed at calling the attention of the public to bullying.

Sexting and Revenge Porn

The Internet never forgets. And that permanent digital record, a blessing when it summons a moment we want to recall with the click of a mouse, can be a weapon in amore sinister hands when it preserves ones we would like to forget. Controlling the distribution of the acts we want back, from mere silly poses for a camera to the most intimate deeds, has become a fact of life in the digital age, taking us into uncharged legal and ethical territory. And few expression of this exploitative power are as disturbing as what is known as revenge porn, the posting online of sexually explicit photos or videos by a former partner seeking retribution.[31]

---

[31] Taylor & Francis: Jonathon W. Penney, (2013) Deleting revenge porn, http://policyoptions.irpp.org/magazines/vive-montreal-libre/penney/

POSTING OF NON-CONSENSUAL REVENGE PORN

This act of publicly distributing intimate photos and videos of a person without the individual's consent is not a new phenomenon. In the 1980s, Hustler Magazine added a section to their magazine and titled it the "Beaver Hunt" described as *a contest that published reader-submitted images of naked women. Beaver Hunt photos were often accompanied by details about the woman: her hobbies, her sexual fantasies, and sometimes her name. "*[32] It does not take a stretch of the imagination to believe at least some were stolen photos published by an ex without the permission of the woman. In fact, many women did sue Hustler for illegally publishing their photos.[33] [34] [35]

Where online revenge porn differs from Beaver Hunt and the like is the mass scale of online distribution[36]. As I stated in the introduction, one of the law enforcement investigative services my company operates is www.Cyberbully.watch; through our research we have found cases of victims of revenge porn of all age groups, starting at the very young middle school age through senior citizens. There is no age limit to this problem, and it is more prevalent than you would guess, and its effects have been seen to be disastrous causing public embarrassment, loss of employability for adults, and has resulted in many suicides.

To understand the devastating effects of non-consensual revenge porn and avoid being numbed by the pool of statistics, it is essential to

---

[32] Robert Rosen, Beaver Street: A History of Modern Pornography: From the birth of phone sex to the skin mag in cyberspace: An investigative memoir.
[33] Ursula Ashby, Plaintiff-appellant, v. Hustler Magazine, Inc., Defendant-appellee, 802 F.2d 856 (6th Cir. 1986)
[34] Faloona v. Hustler Magazine, Inc., 607 F. Supp. 1341 (N.D. Tex. 1985)
[35] Gallon v. Hustler Magazine, Inc., 732 F. Supp. 322 (N.D.N.Y 1990)
[36] Robert Rosen, Beaver Street: A History of Modern Pornography: From the birth of phone sex to the skin mag in cyberspace: An investigative memoir.

paint a scenario of how a typical revenge porn bullying plays out with a fictional character of Sadie:

> Sadie is a thirteen-year-old girl who attends a local high school with her sister. From birth, her parents have always told her she is beautiful, but Sadie continues to doubt them because she doesn't feel her body is the right shape or size.
>
> At school, Sadie does not have too many friends and is most times confined to stay with the unpopular kids at the farthest tables in the cafeteria. After a while, she comes in contact with Fred, a classmate of Sadie's sister who begins to tell her she is beautiful. At first, Sadie experiences a kind of mixed feeling because no other schoolmate has voiced the same thought since she has been in the school. Then, slowly, her confusion turns to little delight at finally being recognized by the opposite sex for being beautiful. After this first touch between Sadie and Fred, Sadie makes increased efforts to look good when she is going to school for the next couple of days, and Fred makes sure the stream of compliments continues to roll in.
>
> After a while, Fred asks for Sadie's phone number and social media handles to continue talking after school. Sadie does not read any negative meaning to this request and immediately grants his wish. From that point, the relationship between the two of them begins to blossom. At first, their chats comprise of a couple of nervous pleasantries which Sadie is delighted to have because Fred seems to be

the only boy that ever chats with her. Then, as time progresses, Fred becomes bolder, and the chats become more engaging with terms of endearment such as "babe" being used. The duo then begins to share jokes about other people, discuss popular celebrities, and comfort each other when any of them is down with pain.

Following three months of chatting, on a particular night when Sadie is within her room, a text comes in from Fred requesting Sadie to send a picture of her breasts. At first, she is confused about the request, and when she prods Fred tells her everything is fine. He assures her every other person in the school is doing it, and it is not weird at all. To confirm what he says, he sends a shirtless picture of himself. At this junction, Sadie does not know how to proceed because her parents had warned her of sexting. However, she ponders this is the first real request Fred has asked from her and fears upsetting her only male friend. She then fantasizes Fred asks her to become his girlfriend and then proceeds to take a picture of her breasts. When she sends the image to Fred, she is afraid he would find them unattractive and then sighs with relief when he texts back they look great.

After the first episode passed, Fred continues to request more pictures of Sadie's breasts and then requests she send a full nude photo to him. At this point, Sadie does not find it odd again. Instead, it has become an exciting game she thinks is just being played by herself and Fred.

As time goes on, Sadie begins to enjoy her newfound admiration from boys and starts texting other boys in the school seeking even more attention. When Fred finds out, he is jealous of her actions and thinks her texting other boys is a betrayal. In his rage, he goes online and posts dozens of her naked photographs under a headline of "Johnsonville High School: Sadie's fat and ugly body."

Word quickly makes it around the school, and everyone is talking behind her back. She knows what is going on but is powerless to stop it. From this point on, Sadie's grades begin to drop; she loses her appetite. She begs her parents to let her switch schools but will not tell them why due to embarrassment; they deny her request. Eventually, she commits suicide to escape the horror and embarrassment she experiences at school.

The above scenario featuring Sadie and Fred depicted here, though fictional, is one that is comparable to things real high school girls go through frequently. In many instances, the victim shows signs of not being loved.[37] The victim may suffer from a case of rejection within the school, may be the victim of constant rumors, or feel uncomfortable in her own body.

---

[37] Chiarini, Annmarie. (November 19, 2013). I was a victim of revenge porn. I don't want anyone else to face this.
https://www.theguardian.com/commentisfree/2013/nov/19/revenge- porn-victim-maryland-law-change

It should be made clear while my fictional story above showed a female victim, either gender can be a victim, and the storyline could easily be reversed with the same outcome.

SEXTING

This is a crude term that is taken from two keywords 'sex' and 'texting.' In its most basic definition, it means the act of sending sexually explicit text messages, photographs, or videos between two or more people. While sexting may be a new name that may not be known by many, the occurrence is not a new one[38]. Think of Polaroid instant pictures back in the 80s and 90s and sharing those photos with a lover. It is the same concept, however mobile connected devices such as iPhone and Androids come equipped with a high-resolution digital camera by persons of all ages is now how the pictures and messages are being shared.

Within kids of all age groups, sexting is part of the many activities and are regarded as being 'hip' and a reluctance to engage in it may result in the kid being tagged 'soft' and 'uncool'. In these instances, peer pressure plays a huge role in pushing kids into the act of sexting even though they may not be initially interested. According to a 2015 survey of about 1,606 respondents, 61% stated at one point in their lives they had taken nude pictures or videos of their bodies and sent them to other people. Then, within the same demographic, about 361 people stated they had been victims of revenge porn.[39]

---

[38] Robert Rosen, Beaver Street: A History of Modern Pornography: From the birth of phone sex to the skin mag in cyberspace: An investigative memoir.

[39] Chiarini, A. (2013, November 19). I was a victim of revenge porn. I don't want anyone else to face this | Annmarie Chiarini.
https://www.theguardian.com/commentisfree/2013/nov/19/revenge-   porn-victim-maryland-law-change

I am not here to judge nor encourage you to pass judgment upon those that choose to share sexually explicit photos of themselves with others whom they are intimate. I am not ignorant enough to believe educators or parents can stop children from partaking in sexting. I do, however, feel with the right approach the children can be educated to the risks associated with sexting and with improved law enforcement investigative tools similar to those provided by stockNum Systems[40] we can heavily reduce such cases as our fictional Sadie story above.

SEXTORTION

Sextortion is a twist on sexting and revenge porn; it usually involves the use of threats of posting a sexual image online so a person can engage in an activity for revenge purpose or humiliation. This can go in multiple different directions, but the most common are:

- financial extortion - force the victim to pay money to prevent disclosure of sexually explicit material, or

- sexual extortion - forcing the victim to provide more sexually explicit pictures, videos, etc., to prevent public disclosure of sexually explicit material.

According to research carried out by Brookings, more than 60% of the victims of sextortion knew the perpetrator in real life before the victimization began. Concerning the remaining 40%, they met the perpetrator online. In the same research, many respondents showed they were already in a romantic relationship with the perpetrators. After a while, the other partner began to manipulate and humiliate the other through making strange requests for nudes that were later used for extortion.[41]

---

[40] https://www.stocknum.com/industries-we-serve/law-enforcement.html
[41] Wittes, B., Poplin, C., Jurecic, Q., Spera, C., Wittes, B., Poplin, C., Spera, C. (2018, April 20). Sextortion: Cybersecurity, teenagers, and remote sexual assault. http://www.brookings.edu/research/reports2/2016/05/sextortion-wittes-poplin-jurecic-spera

In the same research carried out by the Brookings Institute, it was discovered:

- 54% of the contact between the predators and their victims occurred through social media,

- 41% happened through messaging apps,

- 23% through video voice calls,

- 12% through emails,

- 9% through dating apps,

- and 4% through gaming platforms.

The research revealed when the interactions began between the two sides (perpetrator and victim), the perpetrator lied about who they were and most times hinted false impression in over half of the cases. Those lies broke down:

- 45% lied about desiring romantic relationships,

- 39% lied concerning their age,

- 17% lied about their gender,

- 13% lied about being someone the victim knew,

- 21% made other lies about their intentions

- Within face-to-face and online messaging, close to 70% of the respondents provided sexual images to their predators.

When they were queried concerning the reasons for sending the nudes:

- 72% of the victims stated they felt it was okay since they were in a relationship,

- 51% believed they were pressured,

- 15% stated they felt tricked,

- 13% felt threatened and coerced,

- 2% believed they would be paid for the pictures with some believing their images would be utilized for professional modeling purposes. [42]

Research into sextortion further revealed that for 45% of cases, the predators got the images of the victims without the knowledge and consent of the latter. Cases that involved the recording of images through webcam were 18%, while cases of picture taking with mobile phones without permission were right under 10%. In another 8% of the cases, the respondents noted the photos were fake or photoshopped, while the last 5% recorded that the perpetrators hacked into their computer and mobile devices in order to get their pictures or videos.[43]

It is pertinent to note the Brookings Institute research is vital as it identifies the statistics of the demands of the perpetrators.

- According to 51% of the victims, the perpetrator wanted additional sexual images or videos.

- 42% of victims, the perpetrators wanted the victim to stay put in a relationship with the perpetrator or return back after leaving.

---

[42] Wittes, B., Poplin, C., Jurecic, Q., Spera, C., Wittes, B., Poplin, C., Spera, C. (2018, April 20). Sextortion: Cybersecurity, teenagers, and remote sexual assault. http://www.brookings.edu/research/reports2/2016/05/sextortion-wittes-poplin-jurecic-spera
[43] Sextortion. (2017, July 31). https://cyberbullying.org/sextortion

- 28% of victims, the perpetrators wanted the respondents to take new photos with suggested poses.

- 28% of victims, the perpetrators wanted the victims to meet them in person in order to mostly engage them in sexual activities.

- 24% of victims, the perpetrators wanted to meet the victim online in order to initiate sexual activity.

- 10% of victims, the perpetrators wanted the victims to physically harm themselves.

- 7% of victims, the perpetrators wanted the victims to take sexual pictures of other people.[44]

In a deviant fashion, many perpetrators threaten to do many things to victims if their wishes are not carried out. In about 44% of the cases, the perpetrators actually carried out their threats, which included:

- 71% stalked their victims with regular unwanted online and phone contact

- 45% began to send sexual images of the victims to people the victims knew

- 40% began to post the sexual pictures online

- 26% posted the personal details of the victim along with the images they posted[45]

---

[44] Sextortion. (2017, July 31). https://cyberbullying.org/sextortion
[45] Sextortion. (2017, July 31). https://cyberbullying.org/sextortion

Cyberstalking

Stalking by definition is the giving of unwanted and obsessive attention to a specific person. It can take different forms, some of which includes following or continually keeping eyes on the person. This can take place in the physical world or online, with the main difference being the dependence on online technology; seemingly innocent pieces of information online can be abused to gain more information about an intended victim.

Generally speaking, this behavior threatens or otherwise incites fear, invades the relative right of privacy, and manifest themselves in repeated actions over time.

Do not confuse cyberstalking with searching for an acquaintance on social media. There is a big difference between going on social media to look for information on a new classmate or a new roommate. As a matter of fact, a person's profile and news feed on social media are made public for people to have access to them. Cyberstalking is a different ball game; it usually involves unhealthy intentions which if used in a particular way can, of course, lead to bullying.

Although stalking has been a phenomenon that has been around for decades, laws prohibit it at the state and national level and sanctions for violation of these laws, cyberstalking can be quickly done given the use of the ever-present Internet platforms and resources to help achieve the victimization. In fact, because of the undoubted overlap of both social media and 24/7 connectivity, it is difficult for the two to be conceptually distinguished. Cyberstalking is considered a form of emotional assault; it has received a lot of attention over the years. Most of the cases of cyberstalking lead to suicide attempts and sexual assaults; this is why it is considered a cybercrime in most countries. While some of these countries have laws that are unreformed, others have introduced laws tailored for cyberstalking only.

Examples of Cyber Stalking

CATFISHING

Catfishing is rampant on social media sites like Facebook and Instagram. It is somewhat like impersonation, a situation where a stalker creates a fake account on a social media platform and then approach their targets as either a friend of a friend or a complete stranger. Most catfishers are not bullies, but the possibility cannot be ruled out.

Back in 2006, Megan Meier, who was 13 at the time, started an online relationship with someone claiming to be a boy her age[46]. His online name was Josh Evans, and the two chatted with each other online for about a month. They didn't exchange phone numbers because the boy alleged he had no cell phone, so the internet was their meeting place. Their conversations became very intimate and from Megan's perspective, she thought of Josh as her boyfriend.

Later on that same year, Josh sent a message to Megan via MySpace, telling her he doesn't want to be friends with her anymore because she is not nice to her friends at school. What followed after the message was bash boards and bulletins circulating MySpace[47]. Megan, who was young and heartbroken by this person she thought she knew, hung herself in her bedroom. Megan's body was discovered by her mother, who couldn't do anything to save her daughter.[48]

A few weeks after Megan was buried, it was discovered Josh Evans did not exist in real life. The said account was created by Megan's adult neighbor Lori Drew. Lori was the mother of a girl Megan's age; according to her, she created the account to keep an eye on what Megan was saying about her daughter. Lori was arrested and charged with violations of the Computer Fraud and Abuse Act (CFAA) over the alleged cyberbullying, but she was eventually acquitted.[49]

---

[46] Understanding the Megan Meier Case, https://cyber.laws.com/megan-meier-case
[47] Vague Cyberbullying Law, NY Times, SEPT. 7, 2009
https://www.nytimes.com/2009/09/08/opinion/08tue2.html
[48] Suicide of Megan Meier, Wikipedia,
https://en.wikipedia.org/wiki/Suicide_of_Megan_Meier
[49] United States v. Drew, 259 F.R.D. 449 (C.D. Cal. 2009)
https://en.wikipedia.org/wiki/United_States_v._Drew

MONITORING LOCATION CHECK-INS ON SOCIAL MEDIA

Reports show most children that are cyberstalked are those that constantly geo-tag themselves on their social media pages. A child can be easily threatened by anybody that knows where he/she spends time outside of school. For example, a bully can simply threaten his victim by telling him about all the places he goes to, and this will put a sense of burden on the victim who will always be on the lookout for danger. So if a child is adding location check-ins to their Facebook and Instagram posts, they are making it easier for cyberstalkers to track them.

STALKING VIA GOOGLE MAPS STREET VIEW

With Google Maps Street View, cyberstalkers can see precisely what the house looks like without even going into the victims' neighborhood and drawing attention. In addition, cyberstalkers can virtually explore the environment: houses, cameras, and alleys surrounding them to get a sense of where their victim lives in.

HACKING OF DEVICE (CAMERA, VIDEOS, DATA, ETC.)

Hacking or hijacking the camera of a mobile phone or computer is one of the most futile methods used by cyberstalkers to invade privacy.[50] This used to be a tough task to accomplish, but these days all it requires is to get someone to download a malware virus. This malware is purposefully created to allow unauthorized access to a

---

[50] Cyber pervert hacked unsuspecting victims' webcams and watched them having sex, The Telegraph, Oct 2015 https://www.telegraph.co.uk/news/uknews/crime/11918018/Cyber-pervert-hacked-unsuspecting-victims-webcams-and-watched-them-having-sex.html

webcam without the owner's knowledge. Hijacking a webcam is an invasion of privacy of the highest magnitude. Many preteen and teenage victims have been caught in private moments changing their clothes, taking a shower, etc with their laptops open playing music.

Cyberbullies that are classmates usually do not have the technical expertise to implement such a hack; these are usually isolated to online sexual predators.[51] For such a hack to take place, the victim needs to be tricked into downloading an application online and grant the application access to your device. Sometimes this is done by cloaking the application as a pirated movie or music album or sometimes as a free software program claiming to provide a different but legitimate purpose to the user. By this single act, they will have access to your photo gallery, video recordings, and even your passwords.

After being hacked, many of these cases start out with an innocent video or picture of the victim changing their clothes and a threat of, "*I will show your naked pix to everyone at your school.*" The predator will then convince the victim to take more explicit photos or videos. Once the victim complies with the demand for more explicit material, a new round of even more explicit requests all with the threat of, "*Do you want me showing mommy and daddy what a bad little girl you were last night?*" Thus begins a vicious cycle that can be very difficult for the victim to extricate themselves from.

ADDRESSING CYBERSTALKING

Cyberstalking will remain a societal menace for a long time, and bullies will continue to use it on unsuspecting victims. However, to tackle it there is a need for extreme caution to be taken.

---

[51] Arrest made in Miss Teen USA Cassidy Wolf 'sextortion' case, CNN,
https://www.cnn.com/2013/09/26/justice/miss-teen-usa-sextortion/index.html

Precautions should be taken of the activities that are made public. Geo-tagging and location check-ins should be used only when necessary, especially for someone who is prone to cyberstalking. If you are using an iPhone or Android device, review your privacy settings and disable location services for apps you do not want sharing your GPS location information.

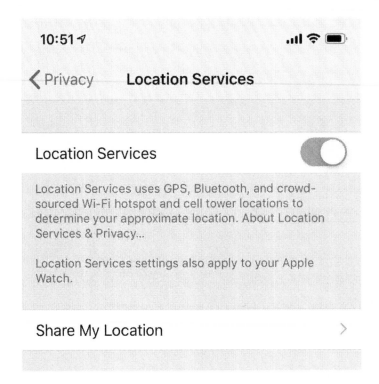

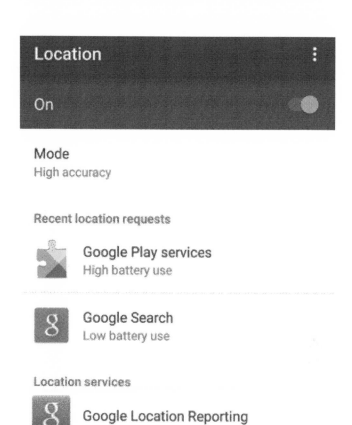

Parents and educators should also do well to always educate their children on the importance of controlling what they put into their devices.

THREATS OF VIOLENCE

Due to the fact the internet is highly accessible, it has led to the daily increase of cyberbullying, especially among young people. With the use of smartphones, computers and other electronic devices, they have access to email, social media sites (Facebook, Twitter, and Instagram), chat rooms, messaging apps (Facebook Messenger, Skype, WhatsApp), online gaming websites and so on, where cyberbullying can take place. One of the forms of cyberbullying is threats of violence.

A cyber threat is defined as any intimidating material online that indicates the author or offender may commit an act of violence, suicide, or self - harm. Online violence and abuse against kids takes many different forms. It may include direct and indirect violent threats such as physical or sexual threats.

Most of the school kids who have had experiences of abuse or harassment online said they were threatened with physical or sexual violence (directly or indirectly). Threat violence is an offline or online behavior that leads to an attack on an individual or a group's well-being (physical, psychological, emotional). What distinguishes the online form of this violence from the traditional forms (offline violence) is a significant portion of the behavior takes place online, although it may then be transferred to offline situations. Cyber violence may, therefore, have a physical component, but it does not in all senses have to and much of the harm caused by online threats of violence is psychological and/or emotional. Cyber violence may be targeted at individuals or groups; with the latter being a more characteristic target of cyber violence when compared to offline. This is due to the ease with which a single perpetrator can gather information and make contact with large numbers of people on the Internet, and it can have far-reaching effects.

Threats of violence have a substantial negative impact on kids. Psychologically, it brings about fear and anxiety in them leading to depression, isolation, and post-traumatic stress disorder (PTSD). This also affects the victim's social life (interaction with family members, peer groups, and so on). As a result of this, the child withdraws and becomes more secretive, keeping more to his or herself. Furthermore, there is a considerable decline in the victim's academic performance; he or she will have no interest in studying and engaging in extracurricular activities.

If as a parent or educator, you notice these changes in your kids, you should be concerned and take specific measures to handle the situation. Talk to the child, make him or her feel comfortable, and when the child opens up to you, listen without judgment. Do not blame or attempt to jump in and 'solve' the problem. Congratulate your child on his or her courage and discuss things that hopefully will help the victim get help or fix the problem themselves. If there is evidence of the threats of violence: saved text messages, posts, websites, etc., have your child show these to you and save these for documentation. After, report it to your local law enforcement officials immediately. Parents may also need to set up appointments with the school's counselor or ask the school's counselor for names of therapists who have expertise in working through the effects of the threats of violence on your child depending on how he or she is recovering mentally.

Precaution needs to be taken, so kids are safe from threats of violence. Parents and schools should create awareness among kids on threats of violence in regards to cyberbullying. To do that you need to understand the risks kids might face. Provide education on this topic, how it can affect children, and how it can be avoided. Kids need to be made aware of social media threats. Monitor Internet access for children and what they make public. It's important to know what kids are putting on the web and to make sure they don't disclose personal and private information such as their addresses, telephone numbers, or school names.

Similarly, children need to avoid communicating with people they don't know; this is another way to stay safe. Maintain an open parent-child dialogue. A free, natural conversation between parents and children helps them to feel the family bond they need when it becomes necessary to turn to an adult. Perhaps the most crucial way to deal with these issues is to establish a relationship of trust. It cannot be overstated the importance of on-going open dialog on the cyber-universe.

Online security conversations should start from the moment kids start roaming the internet. Explaining the physical and digital world are two sides of the same coin, and just like the real world, the online world is home to safe as well as unsafe things. Use computer safety solutions. It is pertinent to note tools of a technological nature can play significant roles in protecting equipment, user data, and the likes.

When a safety solution is used, for instance, the computer will be protected from incidents of invasive hacking that are aimed at stealing information from the computer. Also, the tools have unique parental features that enable parents to censor the content their children are exposed to. Options such as setting up restricted children's user accounts are designed to support you in your mission to help your kids make safe and productive use of the internet. There are various ways to deploy such controls, including at the level of the network, device, or application. In short, these features can filter and block low content for the ages, limit the information you have shared, and keep tabs on children's screen time. They can also keep activity logs allowing you to get an insight into what type of online content your children have access or have tried accessing. Online protection for children might appear to be a technological problem, but it is a parental problem at heart. This is just another way to look after them, to mirror your care in the real world, and to complement them.

Places of Cyberbullying

In this chapter, we are going to go over a few websites where cyberbullying take place. It is not my place nor the goal of this chapter to pass judgment on the morality of these websites; I will leave that up to you. I only highlight these sites so you can get a better understanding of the context of some cyberbullying.

BASH BOARDS: FACEBOOK, 4CHAN, REDDIT, AND OTHERS

Bash boards are becoming popular in recent times. Bash boards are online newsletters where young people post whatever they want. Over the past decade, bash boards have been frequently used by both cyberbullies and peer groups of young people. This makes it somewhat easy to bully someone online as anything posted on it is open to the general public. The cyberbully publishes negative and devaluing information concerning the target victim. Before you know it, everyone has that information. Bash boards have continually seen criticism from parents, so they are less frequent when compared to the way it used to be. Common bash boards are found on Facebook and Reddit under terms like "Confessions of XX" with XX being a locality or school name. An example of a local one where I live is "Confessions and Rants of Page County, Va"

REVENGE PORN: PORNHUB AND MOTHERLESS.COM

PornHub is a popular online adult website that mostly has content from professional adult studios and performers. They also have a section where users can submit content, and this is regularly abused by users to submit revenge porn. With gallery post titles such as "Florida State University College Girl Private Nude Photos Exposed" and "Barley Legal HS Senior Slut Exposed" it does not take a Ph.D. in linguistics to know these galleries were posted for revenge. Overall PornHub does a pretty decent job of removing content that is reported as revenge.

While PornHub is a website you probably have heard of, one you may not be familiar with is Motherless.com. This is one of the leading websites dedicated to the anonymous posting of sexually explicit photos and videos. Technically the website is not for "revenge" postings, and they state in their Terms of Service not to post revenge. The truth is, the site is chock full with millions of photos and videos that are all user submitted with questionable legal status at best. This site is probably one of the more seedier websites on the web, without stepping onto the Darkweb.

These are only a few of the thousands of websites allowing posting of revenge style pornography and requires the use of advanced technology to help law enforcement track down and remove illegally posted non-consensual revenge style porn.[52]

---

[52] stockNum Systems: Law Enforcement Solutions - https://www.stocknum.com/industries-we-serve/law-enforcement.html

How Bullying Does Harm

Have you ever wondered why there is a growing incidence of child suicide in schools nowadays, or what is it about bullying that makes it so adverse a victim would seek death as a means of escape? According to the Center for Disease Control and Prevention, suicide is one of the leading causes of death among adolescents, and general suicide rates have increased steadily from the year 1999.[53] The truth is when it comes to bullying, there are so many things that could go wrong and spiral out of control because at every point in time, bullying is accompanied by moodiness and excessive thinking, and when this is not controlled abruptly, it could birth several issues one of which could result in suicidal ideation.

Throughout one's life it is normal for an individual to develop feelings of frustration, disappointment, and despair, but unlike these everyday instances, cyberbullying is inescapable; it is also accompanied by feelings of frustration, disappointment, or depression, and when this happens, it may cultivate suicidal ideation in the mind of the individual.

Surprisingly, the link between bullying and suicide is not so straightforward. Logically, the victims of bullying are supposed to be

---

[53] Suicide Among Youth | Gateway to Health Communication | CDC
https://www.cdc.gov/healthcommunication/toolstemplates/entertainmented/tips/SuicideYouth.html

the ones affected by suicidal ideation; however, the prospect of suicidal ideation affects both the bully and the victim. This is because bullying itself as an act may be due to several issues some of which might be genetic or environmentally disposed. Bullying might be a manifestation of a troubled environment or even a broader matter relating to the biological composition of the person. This implies that nature and nurture plays a significant role in the development of bullying habits. The continuous act of bullying by a child against his peers if left unchecked may eventually drive the bully into a dark place where they are left questioning the meaning and essence of life.

As human beings, we are consistently in pursuit of meaning. In fact in most situations, a purpose is the difference between happiness and sadness or between cheerfulness and depression. Suicidal ideation is usually developed slowly as an individual loses a sense of meaning. When life becomes meaningless, existence is questioned. Bullying messes up the bully's perspective about life. It corrupts their mindset of what human communication and relationships should be until they are lonely and devoid of meaningful friends because their friends will have distanced themselves after being repeatedly bullied. This is why when bullying is perpetrated for years, both the bully and the victim can become exposed to suicidal ideation either in the short or long run.

It is important to note sometimes kids, just like adults, are just jerks. It is an unfortunate aspect of life, but some people are just not very pleasant. Not all children that are mean to other children require psychological intervention, the key as an educator is to identify the students that have the warning signs of being a bully or being a victim.

In the discussion about the link between bullying and suicide, it is also important to clarify, thankfully, bullying does not always lead to suicide. A bullying victim does not necessarily always turn to self-harm to escape; in most cases that suicide does take place, it is the result of multiple factors. Just as there are many cases of bullying victims committing suicide, there are also numerous cases of bullying victims not committing suicide. What is certain though is the fact bullying can increase the possibility of an individual committing suicide. Bullying makes one feel unwanted and unloved, and it can have a significant effect on the social life of the victim. Indeed, it is not just the social life of the victim that could be affected; literally, every aspect of the life of the victim can potentially be affected. Suicide is a public health concern that may affect anyone regardless of whether they have been bullied before, have bullied others themselves, or never been involved in either situations. Suicide has become a commonly associate construct with bullying these days that a word has been coined for it. Bullycide is the word used to describe suicidal attempts resulting from past or previous bullying experiences[54].

Why can bullying lead to suicide? This is a big question that has been subject to empirical scrutiny and investigation for a long time, and even more studies about it are ongoing. One thing we already know about bullying though is the fact it usually involves physical, verbal, or emotional aggressive behavior from one person to another. That is obvious; the key is how do we differentiate between children being mean and children intent on the direct harm of other children that could result in self-harm or suicide? This question is far more challenging to come to a concrete answer.

The very same way sickness threatens the physical and general wellbeing of the individual, bullying also endangers the physical, mental, cognitive, and emotional welfare of an individual. Naturally, when the physical component of an individual is damaged, they may

---

[54] Deborah Serani Psy.D, Psychology Today,
https://www.psychologytoday.com/us/blog/two-takes-depression/201806/bullycide

still find the will to cope by building up their emotional capacity to deal with the resulting stress that the damage in their body will introduce to their lives. This is why there are so many physically challenged people doing well for themselves in the society today. Many have gone on to achieve success and fame in one profession or another because, rather than cave into the challenge, they have mustered the courage to live and enjoy life just like every other person.

A human being is composed of several components which function together. They operate in a state of homeostasis so when there is a deficit or imbalance in one part, whether temporarily or permanently, the other parts pick up the slack to keep the individual functioning as they should. One reason why bullying is so deadly is it can damage the individual physically, mentally, and emotionally all at one time.

As a result of the breakdown of their mental, physical, and affective domains, the victim may even be disinterested in fighting back no matter how reliable and efficient the support structure of family and friends are they have around them. This is why even if the victim is surrounded by loving parents and teachers and officials with a strong stance against bullying in any kind, they may still find it challenging to come forward to expose their bullies. They have been battered and broken down by the repeated acts of bullying and have reached a state of hopelessness that even if help comes their way, they will likely be unreceptive of it by then.

There is more to bullying than meets the eye. A lot goes in the mind of both the bully and their victims that is difficult to conceptualize what is going on behind the scenes. The lack of interest in seeking help is one of the reasons behind the high rate of suicide among school-aged children, not just in the developed nations but also in the developing ones. The children also have a feeling the adult will not believe them, so rather than report to authorities or even to their parents at home several victims might elect to handle it themselves. Some might want to avoid being perceived as weak by their bullies and would instead continue being abused, and this could result in an unfortunate ending. The belief in ignoring and overlooking hurtful and aggressive behaviors of others has certainly done more harm than good as it has only compounded the problem rather than ease it.

In most cases, silence means approval, and when the victim willfully accepts aggressive acts meted out to them by others, they are indirectly urging on the bully to continue his bullying acts towards them. When the victims remain silent, it might intimidate the bully into thinking he's not doing enough and needs to do more to be felt by his target. The increase in their aggression towards the victim may push both the victim and the bully further into the darkness of depression and subsequent suicidal ideation.

Anything done consistently will develop into a habit. When habits are not quickly curtailed, they may mesh into the person's personality. With proper intervention, even a deeply ingrained habit can be changed.[55]

When it comes to character, the individual difference is a significant factor. Some individuals possess a dominant personality, and some possess a submissive nature. The disposition of individuals determines how they respond to situations. This is why it is easier for some to overcome bullying, while it might be difficult for some to deal with the consistent acts of bullying. This is perhaps the main reason why scholars have looked into the gender perspective to bullying. It is

---

[55] Jason Selk, Forbes Magazine, Habit Formation: The 21-Day Myth, https://www.forbes.com/sites/jasonselk/2013/04/15/habit-formation-the-21-day-myth/

suggested suicide resulting from bullying is more predominant among males than among females.[56]

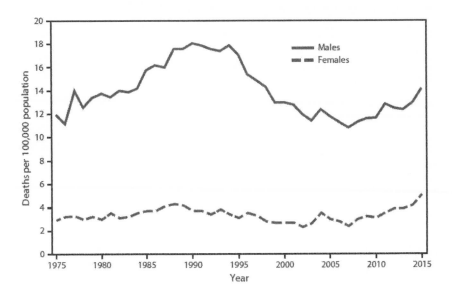

* Rates are per 100,000 population.

† Suicides are identified with International Classification of Diseases (ICD) 8th Revision codes E950–E959 for 1975–1978; ICD 9th revision codes E950–E959 for 1979–1998; and ICD 10th revision codes U03, X60–X84 and Y87.0 for 1999–2015. In 1975, in the United States, there were 1,289 suicides among males and 305 suicides among females aged 15–19 years. In 2015, there were 1,537 suicides among males and 524 among females aged 15–19 years.

The suicide rate for males aged 15–19 years increased from 12.0 to 18.1 per 100,000 population from 1975 to 1990, declined to 10.8 by 2007, and then increased 31% to 14.2 by 2015. The rate in 2015 for males was still lower than the peak rates in the mid- 1980s to mid-

---

[56] American Foundation for Suicide Prevention, Suicide Statistics, https://afsp.org/about-suicide/suicide-statistics/

1990s. Rates for females aged 15–19 were lower than for males in the same group but followed a similar pattern during 1975–2007. Rates increased from 2.9 to 3.7 from 1975 to 1990 followed by a decline from 1990 to 2007. The rates for females then doubled from 2007 to 2015 from 2.4 to 5.1. The rate in 2015 was the highest for females for the 1975–2015 period.[57]

This goes against the popular belief males have a higher potential to cope with bullying than females; however, it is interesting to note female rates of teen suicides are climbing at a higher rate than males and is predicted to surpass males within a few years.[58]

It is not entirely a strange phenomenon; the reason why suicide resulting from bullying is common among school children. The emotional distress that accompanies bullying can be too much for some children to handle; even adults sometimes break down due to the emotional turmoil that results from bullying. Imagine continually feeling sad and lonely; regardless of age, it is a feeling no one deserves to have. Love and acceptance make a whole lot of difference among human beings. We are social beings, and we thrive based on our conversations and interactions with one another. Children are still developing in all facets of life, and this is why no child deserves to be bullied. There is a link between the physical and mental components of the body. Bullying is a form of physical and psychological warfare, and the effect is felt in both aspects. This explains why consistent acts of bullying may lead to the development of physical symptoms such as headaches, stomach aches, etc. These are awful experiences that may

---

[57] *QuickStats:* Suicide Rates for Teens Aged 15–19 Years, by Sex — United States, 1975–2015. MMWR Morb Mortal Wkly Rep 2017;66:816. DOI: http://dx.doi.org/10.15585/mmwr.mm6630a6

[58] U.S. Suicide Rates Are Rising Faster Among Women Than Men, https://www.npr.org/sections/health-shots/2018/06/14/619338703/u-s-suicides-rates-are-rising-faster-among-women-than-men

accompany bullying and is precisely what makes it unbearable for most school-aged children.

Delay in taking action against bullying is dangerous. The best time to act is the very first time the act is perpetrated. Making strong action against bullying is a necessary step to take for both the bully and the victim. Aggressive children have a natural tendency to become bullies; educators and parents must take notice to ensure they work towards teaching their children to treat other people equally regardless of their race, color, gender, sexual orientation, religion, or anything else that makes a person differ from another. Love is a natural antidote to bullying because bullying in itself is a form of hatred. Parents must take the lead in showing respect to their children as children learn from what they see, how they are treated, and are more attuned to take on the characters of either or both of their parents. So many lives have already been lost to bullying, and many have gone down with a range of behavioral, cognitive, and affective problems all because of constant bullying from others around them.

REPUTATION DAMAGE FOR ADULT PROFESSIONAL LIFE

The emergence of cyber technology has given communication a new form and made it easy and fast. With the emergence of wearable mobile technology people are always fully connected to the internet making it possible for the information to be instantly dispersed online and to a broader range of audience than simple word-of-mouth communications of the past. This innovation is beneficial because it helps people to stay connected with friends, family, and the world at large through texts and visuals. Despite the benefits of mobile technology, it is also saddled with negative consequences, because it is possible to disperse information not only instantly and to a broad audience, but also anonymously, which increases the tendency for harmful effects due to harassment especially cyberbullying.

The internet and in turn cyberbullying are not confined to a single geographical area nor are they neatly divisible along territorial boundaries into distinct local networks. People can be subjected to cyberbullying from perpetrators or sites outside geographical boundaries of their local community.

The internet and other digital communications technologies have ways in which people's privacy can be invaded and compromised. This leaves them vulnerable to serious privacy violations through the posting of private, false, humiliating, shameful, and harmful content through social networking websites such as Facebook, Twitter, or YouTube without their consent. This goes a long way to damage their reputations because the extent of reach of the content posted online cannot readily be determined since they are spread instantly and widely and could possibly be reaching global audiences. Also, the permanent nature of online content, as well as the potential for such material to go viral and remain in the public consciousness, shows cyberbullying has substantial long-term damaging effects on people's reputation such as harming future employment prospects and having harmful effects on the individual's physical or mental health. This long-term effect cannot easily be predicted or documented. Judging from reported cases, victims reports, and the study of behavioral patterns of victims, the immediate effects of cyberbullying are well documented, because they can readily be determined. The victims are distressed frequently causes depression as a result. Also, cyberbullying and harassment can lead to suicide.

REPUTATIONAL DAMAGE FOR VICTIMS LATER IN LIFE

A point that cannot be understated is how some cyberbullying released today can stay on the internet and harm someone years down the road. Case in point, pornographic or suggestive photographs uploaded to the internet as revenge will be circulated by countless hands and uploaded to multiple websites. If you successfully remove the photo from one website, it can be easily uploaded to another site. It is like a game of whack a mole. Sadly, the internet never forgets.

REPUTATIONAL DAMAGE FOR BULLIES

Eventually, these children do grow up and enter the adult world and the workforce. Human Resource departments of many organizations weed out prospective applicants who may have been bullies previously. This act is undertaken by a strict search conducted on the online profile of the applicant. If the research process turns out to reveal the applicant as a cyberbully in the past, it would be difficult for such an individual to be hired. The reason is this: organizations are usually interested in keeping a public face that is free of any form of controversy. This is why they organize community service projects aimed at showcasing the company in an excellent public eye. Also if the company were to discover an individual had been a racist in the past who had used racial slurs to cyberbully other people, the company would not accept the individual. The implication of hiring such an individual is the company may be seen as condoning racism, and this may negatively harm the PR of the company.

To identify the magnitude effect of cyberbullying on reputation damages let us take a look at the process of ascending to the top of U.S. Judicial institution, the United State Supreme Court. There are 9 Supreme Court Justices within the country, and the process of becoming a part of them is one of the most stringent. The reason for this is the position is a highly placed one requiring individuals who possess the highest morals. When the President of the United States submits a nomination to the Senate, a thorough research process begins. In-Depth research into the online history of the candidate as well as other parts of the person's life is undertaken to find the smallest speck of wrongdoing in the past.

If the person was discovered to have used an offensive comment about the LGBTQ community in the past, the researchers are sure to dig that information up and would significantly hamper the candidate's chances of being confirmed as a Supreme Court Justice. The reason for this is Justices have to be seen as impartial people that are not pushing the agenda of a particular group. In the scenario described, even though the incident happened 20 years back, the LGBTQ community would claim the candidate is negatively biased to the interests of their community. Such is the nature of the Internet; it neither forgets nor forgives.

Furthermore, as a result of reputation damage many people have engaged in acts of suicide. There have been many people who have committed suicide as a result of the reputation damage which occurred after their acts of bullying were uncovered. Within cases like this, the individual may have built a blossoming career complete with a lucrative job and a good family. However, when news about the person's past bullying activities showed up, they lost their jobs as well as underwent traumatic periods. Negative past details that are uncovered about a successful individual tends to spread fast. For example, in the case of the famous Bill Cosby, news about his previous cases of sexual harassment sent shockwaves across the entire world, and it resulted in his swift fall and later incarceration. There is also the example of Paula Deen using racial slurs that cost her most of her sponsors and her cooking show for a while. In the same way, an individual who may have engaged in bullying acts in the past may encounter such monumental fall from the good graces of the public.

The damaging materials online can stay long after the event and can be used to engage in further victimization of the target each time the content is accessed. Most people who were victims of cyberbullying might end up facing more and worse problematic situations as adults. This is due to the continuous reputational damage whenever the perpetrators or other people revisiting the contents years after the initial upload.

REPUTATION DAMAGE FOR VICTIMS

Cyberbullying makes young people grow to become insecure. Victims continuously feel anxious and on guard at all times. Even when they are not actively being bullied, they are consciously expecting it to start anytime. It leaves the victims in a mental and emotional state of feeling unaccepted, isolated, angry, and withdrawn. The victims are looking for ways of escaping a bully's notice. The victim has stunted development because of the constant tension, and this makes them swear off making new friendships or miss out on taking certain chances that could help their development.

There are many other instances wherein the incidence of cyberbullying damaged the child's reputation as an adult. Since the Internet is a location where the contents are scarcely deleted, the victim of a cyberbullying incident can suffer massive reputation damages. It has been discovered that the uncovering of such an incidence may change the way the adult is being addressed. Also, it may open the adult up for new flows of cyberbullying.

Current Law Summary

The question *"Is cyberbullying a crime?"* is a battle that has raged on within many professional and non-professional circles. While there have been laws that have dealt with the issue of bullying, laws that specifically targeted cyberbullying were vague until the mid-2000s.

Legislators, before this time, were not blind to the rising public incidents of cyberbullying which resulted in severe outcomes like suicides or school shootings. Many legislators at the time grew up in a generation before the internet, and they had limited understanding of the technology.

This cautiousness remains in place within many states. Coming up with cyberbullying laws is left in the enforcement of school authorities. The result of this particular action causes it to be seen as a civil issue and not criminal. The laws in these states specify the school should discipline students in appropriate and measured ways. Many educators have faulted this because of the inability to get an accurate measure of discipline for cyberbullies. They maintain since it is not seen as a criminal action, many students would not understand the gravity of their actions.

All states in the US have already created various criminal harassment and stalking laws that are available for prosecutors to use when charging a suspect, but many of these laws do not cover cyberbullying as a whole.[59]

It is important to note because of the destructive nature of cyberbullying, some prosecutors have been creative in their use of existing laws to prosecute people suspected of cyberbullying. For instance, the statutes that mostly exist on criminal harassment provides a way for charges to be brought in.

In some states in the U.S., there have been newly created cyber harassment statutes that make it possible for online bullies to be charged. Within the broader bullying laws of more than half of U.S. states, cyberbullying is added, or replaced with the term *electronic harassment*. This reflects the progress being made by legislators in general to provide accountability for the incidence of cyberbullying within schools as well as homes.

In all states, except for Montana, the law on Bullying mandates schools should set up formal policies that would aid in the identification of cyberbullying behaviors.[60] Those schools are supposed to discuss the possible formal and informal kinds of disciplinary measures that are to follow the violation of such policies. Many state laws require certain elements, such as a given specific definition of cyberbullying, be added to the policy.

In specific terms, here are some States that have *cyberbully* as part of their laws:

- **New Hampshire** - The *Pupil Safety and Violence Prevention Act*[61] is one that requires every local school board to create a policy of

[59] Summary of US Cyberbullying Laws. https://blog.legalsolutions.thomsonreuters.com/legal-research/summary-us-cyberbullying-laws/
[60] http://mediasmarts.ca/digital-media-literacy/digital-issues/cyberbulling/cyberbulling-law
[61] New Hampshire, TITLE LXII, CRIMINAL CODE, CHAPTER 644, BREACHES OF THE PEACE AND RELATED OFFENSES Section 644:4

student safety and violence prevention. This policy must address the issue of bullying and provides technical assistance. Further, the act requires school employees, in general, to regularly report all information that concerns bullying behavior to the principal of the school. Also, the act provides immunity to the school employee who made the report. This immunity is from any cause of action that arises from the failure of the school to offer remedies to the incident.[62]

- **California** - According to the state law within California, bullying is defined within the context of an educational facility and includes "communication... by the means of an electronic act". Then, the *Safe Place to Learn Act*[63], in addition to other code sections, creates any student's *"inalienable right to attend classes on school campuses that are safe, secure, and peaceful."* This state law makes cyberbullying criminal by stating that the use of *"an electronic communication device"* to make an individual afraid for their life is charged as a misdemeanor. This misdemeanor is punishable by up to one year in jail and/or imposition of a fine up to $1,000.

- **Florida** - In the state of Florida, the *Jeffrey Johnston Stand Up for All Students Act*[64] ensures the prompt protection of students from cyberbullying. According to the Act, bullying of any K-12 student or staff members, with particular reference to cyberbullying as defined as *"bullying through the use of technology or any electronic communication"* is totally prohibited. It is pertinent to note that unlike the act at California, this law

---

[62] http://mediasmarts.ca/digital-media-literacy/digital-issues/cyberbulling/cyberbullying-law
[63] California Code, Education Code - EDC § 234
[64] Florida Statutes, Title XLVIII, Chapter 1006, Sub-section 147, Bullying and harassment prohibited

refrains from including criminal sanctions for acts like this. Instead, the Florida State directs every school district to create policies and engage in swift reporting of bullying cases.

- **Missouri** - According to the Missouri statute, cyberbullying is defined to be bullying "*through the transmission of communication including, but not limited to, a message, text, sound, or images by means of an electronic device.*" Then, the law mandates every school employee is required to ensure swift reporting of every incidence of bullying. The laws proceed to state any individual that utilizes social media to engage in bullying another person with particular emphasis on violent threats may be charged with harassment. In this case, it is known as a Class A misdemeanor. However, in the occasion the victim is seen to be 17 years old or younger while the defendant is 21 or older, it would become an automatic Class D felony. It also becomes a Class D felony if the defendant has already gotten a previous harassment conviction.

To get an exhaustive list of the states that have criminalized the incidence of Cyberbullying along with other states that mandate the schools to take charge, you can check their internet resource.[65]

It is pertinent to note the federal case law grants schools permission to discipline offending students for off-campus behaviors if the action disrupts the learning atmosphere of the school.

PENALTIES FOR BULLYING

We have already covered how many states do not explicitly make Cyberbullying a violation of criminal law; it is vital one examines the kinds of penalties created by some of these states for violators.

---

[65] https://cyberbullying.org/bullying-laws

Because there are no uniform policies created by the states, the penalties are generally wide-ranging just like the state laws themselves. Every state usually develops penalties that are dependent on their applicable laws.

Some of the civil sanctions include school intervention through suspension of the offending student. In some cases where the cyberbullying case is tragic, the student may be expelled from the school.

Within some other states like California where cyberbullying is criminal, the penalties for the felonies range from jail time to payment of fines.

There are some points of dispute within some states because the state did not include criminal charges, yet the state mandates schools to enforce administrative penalties such as suspension or expulsion for cyberbullies. Within such instances, the clash is tagged *administrative vs. criminal sanctions,* and educators generally have proposed arguments in defense of both sides.

SECTION TWO:

Educators

When Should An Educator Intervene?

When the subject of cyberbullying is discussed, the conversation inevitably turns to when an educator should step in. Some supporters argue for prompt intervention at the very first sign of bullying. Others advocate for a more careful approach.

REASONS THE HINDER INTERVENTION

Victims hardly talk about their ordeal

The school environment is one wherein there are many egos and personalities. For teenagers especially, they are at the point where they want to be like adults and handle issues such as bullying and criticism on their own. The negative consequence of this is that they often fail terribly in handling their bullies because they are inexperienced. One of the ways children try to control their bullying experience is by behaving as though the words of the bully do not hurt them.

Cyberbullying accounts are mostly hidden

Bullies seem to understand the fact that their actions are not legal. Even though they may not understand the future consequences and the ripple effect their efforts bring, they do know they are carrying out a devastating course of action against their victims. Because of this, many bullies try as much as possible to hide their activities from the glare of educators. Most educators usually catch on late to the incidence of cyberbullying because they do not know what happens when they are not around. In many cases, bullies choose to carry out their acts in secret places and use fake online personas when cyberbullying their victims.

The workload of the Educator

It is pertinent to note in most instances, the workload of an educator may make it difficult to identify cases of cyberbullying accurately. An educator is an individual who has been tasked with monitoring a large number of school kids, as well as ensuring they are appropriately taught.[66] The process of teaching kids as well as researching on topics may be exhausting for many educators, and it is why some educators are lax in identifying issues some of the kids face. It is also pertinent to note educators are humans who have other needs and concerns outside the school environment. Hence, an educator who is likely experiencing challenges in social life may find it difficult to concentrate on effectively monitoring the school kids.

Feeling of incompetence

Within many instances, it has been discovered some educators may feel incompetent in dealing with cases of cyberbullying. This apparent lack of knowledge of what to do results in a passive stance being adopted by the educator when incidents of cyberbullying begin to display themselves. In some other instances, the educators are not fully aware of the major red flags they are to look forward to when identifying incidents of cyberbullying. When educators display such

---

[66] Steyn, G. M. (2004). Problems of, and support for, beginner educators. Africa Education Review, 1(1), 81-94. doi:10.1080/18146620408566271

ignorance, they tend to misinterpret many schoolchildren behaviors and act in ways that push the victims farther away. For instance, a child who is suffering a terrible case of cyberbullying may show some signs of aggression against authority, and the ignorant educator may interpret this as just a child acting out in class. In such instances, the educator does not take the additional step in trying to identify the root cause of the aggression. If a schoolchild showcases signs of withdrawal, an ill-informed educator may feel the child is passing through a phase which the educator feels powerless to change. Worse still, such an inexperienced educator may chalk it off as a case of *teenage phase*.

RED FLAGS OF CYBERBULLYING

Now that we have identified some of the reasons that make it difficult for educators to act on time; it is essential to know the signs that are indicative of cyberbullying.

The child becomes a loner.

Loneliness should not be confused as a sign of negative reality at all times. In some instances, some school children may exhibit character traits of being introverted, and this means they tend to keep to themselves more often than usual. However, when an educator sees a particular child is displaying intense withdrawal signs, that is out of character for the student, there is a need to be concerned.

Mood swings

Many parents and educators often ignore mood swings within teenagers because such occurrences are misinterpreted. In many occasions parents and educators alike believe the student is exhibiting mood swings because of the physical and hormonal changes the student may be going through. In many occasions, it is vital to know the parent and educator may be right. Adolescence is a stage that usually brings with it mood swings.[67] At that point in their lives, kids are trying to comprehend the phase of growth they are passing through. Because they want to act like adults and are still being restricted by their parents and educators, teenagers may showcase their resistance by showing mood swings at an astonishing rate. Also, mood swings are usually present within teenage romantic relationships as feelings of jealousy, and other mood swings tend to be heightened for them.

For victims of cyberbullying, a calm situation has the potential to quickly escalate into a significant issue within any group setting or personal level. To efficiently narrow down cases of mood swings, educators can pay particular notice to school children who have a history of being calm in class. When the educator notices that a child begins to have violent mood swings, an incidence of cyberbullying should be suspected and appropriate actions need to be taken to diminish it.

Increased stress

Stress is a normal human emotion, yet everyone copes with it in varying degrees. It is not uncommon to see school kids being stressed over things adults would find trivial:

- Children can also be stressed because of certain peer pressures to engage in specific actions the child may find to be conflicting with the child's belief system.[68]

- The child may be stressed if a certain level of academic performance is expected and the child is yet to reach the standard.

[67] Greenspan, S. I., & Pollock, G. H. (1991). Adolescence. Madison, CT: International Universities Press.
[68] MedlinePlus Medical Encyclopedia

- The child may also be stressed when he or she is finding it difficult to make new friends.

Because of these reasons, many educators understand various levels of stress are normal with school children. However, high levels of stress can be induced because of the cyberbullying acts against a victim, and the key is to identify stressors that are out of the ordinary and possibly point towards victimization.

Because the victim finds herself or himself in the same environment as the bully, the stress level would always continue to remain at record highs. Any educator who takes note of a stressed child can assess the level of stress within situations that are not supposed to be stressful. For example, the school cafeteria ought not to be a place where stress is compounded because students are usually there to take meals and loosen up through social banter. If an educator notices a child is stressed within such a place, that is a red flag that ought to be examined. It may be the child is in the same environment with the cyberbully.

A display of aggressive behavior

Children who are victims of cyberbullying have often been found to show higher signs of aggression than healthy children of their age and within their environment. The reason for their lashing out is apparent. The emotional state of the victim is one that is in turmoil, and in many instances, the attempt to cover up being a victim leads to occasions when the tempers of the child would flare up. Educators are always trained to keep a mental record of the personality behaviors of the school children they are in charge. When an educator notices a usually quiet and peaceful child has become prone to lashing out at authorities and classmates, it is vital that a critical examination is undertaken into the causes of such action.

Before we proceed, it is essential to identify the actual signs of depression induced by bullying and separate that from other causes. Depression manifests with symptoms of persistent sadness, signs of restlessness, general lack of enthusiasm in activities, cases of chronic fatigue, etc. Educators should always be careful to take note of every warning stated here because they are the effects of cyberbullying.

Many victims of cyberbullying often spend nights crying and having difficulty sleeping. Since they mostly do not think of reporting such cases to adults who can help, the victims accumulate fatigue in overthinking about how to scale through cyberbullying incidents. The victims do not have anything to be happy, since they are helpless in confronting their bullies. Also, since their bullies are within the same environment, the victim finds it difficult to show signs of hope. Any educator that notices a sharp drop in the interest from the student towards a particular subject ought to be concerned.

Depression is a state that is very dangerous to the mental health of both school kids and adults. This is the reason why such cases have to be quickly brought to the attention of the school guidance counselor. Within many instances of depression, which are left untreated, the victim may end up viewing suicide as the only option to escape.

The victim may skip school

Many educators have realized some students are not easily motivated by the thought of being within the school environment. These sets of students have already been identified as those that play hooky from school, and this point does not concern them.

On the other hand, educators know the set of students who obviously enjoy school and normally do well in their studies. When this second category begins to skip school, there is a cause for alarm. Victims of cyberbullying desperately want to avoid any situation of physical contact with their bullies and will skip school if it is the only avenue for them.

In the case of cyberbullying, the victimized child may begin to daily pester the parents or guardians for a transfer to a new school. In many occasions, however, the request of such children is refused by the parents, and this may result in the child's refusal to go to school. When an educator notices a regular pattern of absence from a previously enthusiastic child, it is vital the parents be contacted. This should also be followed up by an inquiry conducted on the classmates of the child. In many cases, the root cause of absence is the perpetual fear of the bully, as well as the stinging rumors the victim has to endure.

A significant drop in grades

Emotional stability is often linked to academic excellence within any environment. The same argument is applicable in reverse, as lack of emotional stability is a factor that brings failure. For many victims of cyberbullying, fear and increased anxiety are two eternal realities they have to deal with at every point of their stay within the school environment.

Fear of the school bully and how their grades would turn out, and then there is anxiety over the way the entire school population would react to rumors that are being peddled concerning the victim. When the two ingredients of fear and anxiety are combined, they create a perfect recipe for academic disaster. Hence, a student who has always maintained good grades with *A's* for a long time may suddenly become a *D* student due to lack of focus. In many instances, it is quite unfortunate some educators place such sharp drops to other reasons apart from cyberbullying. However, it is a red flag that should always be taken into consideration. Another vital red flag which should be noted is when the educator notices a sharp downward spike in the grade due to lack of enthusiasm shown in a group activity. The victim may be disinterested because of the perpetual fear of being within groups.

The victim stops Participating in Social Activities

Victims of cyberbullying have suffered a damaging blow to their self-esteem, and this makes it difficult for them to be excited in engaging in any social activity. When such activities come up, it is difficult to convince the student to take part in them. An educator who notices this change should be quick in understanding it may be a red flag.

The victim hurts self

As we have stated previously in this book, victims who suffer extreme cases of cyberbullying sometimes begin to explore the option of suicide. One noticeable trait that may reveal if a victim is engaging in self-harm is through the writings of the child. If the educator notices a particular child loves writing or writing assignments but there is now a drastic change in the child's writing style to glorify self-harm then something will have to be done. This does not mean all children with a vivid and somewhat dark imagination are a danger. I am sure Quentin Tarantino had some very *colorful* stories written in his creative writing classes.

Educators can also take a cue on this by noticing when kids who use to wear t-shirts and shorts most of the time are now always wearing clothing that is aimed at covering their arms and legs. The child may be intent on covering up marks of self-inflicted harm. An educator who observes this can work with friends of the victim who would be willing to expose the actions to help the victim. The educator can also notify the child's parents of possible self harm suspicions.

The victim suddenly changes friends

Friendships may be a thing of beauty that may turn out to become a curse. Within many instances, friends have turned against each other due to disputes; they then choose to engage in cyberbullying each other. This scenario usually results in a severance of friendship and a kind of dread that resides in the victim when she or he is within the same environment as the former friend(s). It is pertinent for educators to be able to recognize specific radical changes in the friendship of their students and try to have an idea of why the friendship failed. While this may seem to be an impossible task to be undertaken every time, the educator may combine this red flag with another before proceeding to conclude on cyberbullying being the cause. Victims of cyberbullying had often changed friends as well because of a recognized lack of support received from such friends during the period when the victim was being bullied. Just keep in mind, it is normal for children to change friends as they grow up.

Prevention of Cyberbullying

From times past, many educators, boards, and others have tried to come up with a single solution that can put an end to cyberbullying. However, while there has not been one single preventive action, there have been a series of steps educators can take into consideration. It is pertinent to note that not only a preventive course of action must be made without the aid of the parents of school children. This unity of purpose between the educator and parent is needed to strengthen the effectiveness of the actions taken by the educator and parent as well.

IDENTIFICATION OF THE LIKELY CLASS OF VICTIMS

It is essential every educator identify the class of students who are more likely to be victims of cyberbullying. While it is argued this step may ostracize some students, the students identified by the teacher are more likely to be protected by the teacher from incidents of cyberbullying.[69]

The first class of students who are prone to cyberbullying according to the present social atmosphere is LGBTQ kids. Because these kids

---

[69] Betts, L. R. (2016). What Can Be Done About Cyberbullying. Cyberbullying, 103-131. doi:10.1057/978-1-137-50009-0_6

choose to be addressed differently, they would be easy targets within a school filled with kids who are not predominantly LGBTQ.

The second class of students that may be targeted are students with physical disabilities. It is unfortunate there is mostly intolerance within school environments, and this is why such kids are always being focused.

The third set of easy targets are children of an ethnic and religious minorities. For example, in a school that is situated in a predominantly black neighborhood, kids who are not black may be seen as easy targets. The same occurs vice versa in a community dominated by white kids.

The fourth set are children of lower economic class. These children are typically seen as easy targets. The victim may not even know at first they are being cyberbullied due to a lack of ability to be on social media. They may be shown what is being said online by a friend. Identifying the right class of school kids that are prone to be bullied makes it easy for the educator to spot out incidents.

FIGHT FIRE WITH FIRE

While the latest in technology may elude some educators, most of them can easily navigate social media platforms like Facebook, Instagram, SecureTribe, etc. Since cyberbullying occurs online, just like how bullies use fake user accounts, educators could adopt a clandestine profile that would not be easily suspected. When cyberbullying begins, the teacher would be able to identify the victim and provide the necessary help needed. Also, with the monitoring of those spaces, bullies would be identified and promptly dealt with according to school punishment scheme.

Furthermore, educators can engage in monitoring of physical places such as buses, recesses, and free periods where victims are likely to feel more depressed due to the stinging looks they get from other students. A seasoned educator would identify a bully-rich environment, such as the school lunchroom as a place to monitor. Within such a loud environment, it is easy for students to discuss rumors they have heard concerning the victim, and the educator can pick up such stories. Whereas on the internet, cyberbullying is usually at the highest peak; this is where educators need to be versed in the art of observation.

GET THE SUPPORT OF EVERYONE IN THE CAMPAIGN AGAINST CYBERBULLYING

While educators may have some power to deal with cases of cyberbullying within the school environment, what happens when the victim goes home? The cyberbully may be a classmate who usually engages in cyberbullying when he or she gets home. Because of this, a joint effort between educators and parents has to be led for preventing cyberbullying. The parents of the bully and the victim need to work with the educator for this effort to be effective.

WORKING WITH PARENT/GUARDIAN

First, as an educator you can work directly with the parent or guardian of the victim to monitor access to the internet. Cyberbullying usually thrives when the victim continues to access the same platform daily or chat with the bully. The parent would need to be on the alert to identify signs of increased stress and ought to intrude on the privacy of the child if there is a suspicion the child is trying to hide the fact she or he is a victim. If the educator suspects a student is a cyberbully, it would be essential to work with the parent discreetly to identify the online activities of the bully.

WORKING WITH SEASONED PROFESSIONALS

Educators have a responsibility to work with seasoned professionals such as psychologists, computer specialists, cafeteria specialists, school resource officers (SROs), paraprofessionals, and others. Usually, these professionals are closest to victims of cyberbullying and can efficiently provide tips that can help the educator.

For example, the computer specialist would be able to provide information concerning the latest trends of cyberbullying, the best way to maintain vigilance, and how to identify the social networks that bullies meet online.

The psychologist will be able to teach the educator some specific signs being shown by victims and give a good lesson on body behavior of a victim around the cyberbully.

Then, the SROs would be briefed on the law enforcement actions to take when they sense cyberbullying occurring within their school.

There is no single extensive list of professionals that an educator can engage in this joint effort to prevent cyberbullying.

WORKING WITH STUDENTS

When cases of cyberbullying occur, it is not all students that are collectively working against the victim. Though a considerable number may contribute to the cycle of bullying online, there would be others that hate the act. However, it has been discovered many such students are reluctant to become active 'up-standers' that would protect the victim. This reluctance could be narrowed down to a desire not to become another target of cyberbullies. In fighting to prevent cyberbullying, the educator would have to involve this class of students and encourage them to always report such cases to the appropriate authority.

To fully convince students to go against the collective, the educator would need to teach them the adverse effects which cyberbullying has on students in the long run. The educator can begin to create Anti-bullying campaigns on prominent social media spaces where students are. An example may be the use of Twitter to start hashtag campaigns like *#NotoRevengePorn, #NoToCyberBullying,* etc. When these campaigns are created, educators can encourage influential students to popularize them so they would be made popular.

Some middle schools have been successful in bringing in mature college or high school students to speak with the middle schoolers about bullying. This works because the students look up to the "cooler" older students and aspire to be like them. As I am sure you know, you can tell a student something, and it goes in one ear and out the other; however, when an older student says the exact same sentence to the kids, it is more impactful.

RESEARCH ONLINE TO GET RESOURCES

Since the internet is the medium through which cyberbullies get information on how to immortalize their actions, it is logical for educators to take advantage of numerous anti-Cyberbullying toolkits that are available online. Thankfully, cyberbullying is a vice educators have made a general stance against. There are multiple online journals filled with studies that are vital in the fight against Cyberbullying. Also, there are online groups for educators to interact with each other to jointly share ideas that have been tested and trusted. An educator would also be able to discard old techniques based upon discussions with different educations. One online location where teachers can get enough resources, as well as relevant emergency contact details is the National Education Association. At this site, there is the availability of lesson plan collections, activities meant to teach against bullying, quizzes, and other information. All these essential resources are available free of charge. There are also online tools such as Cyberbully.watch that helps educators and parents fight back.

CREATE A CULTURE OF RESPECT

Equality - Every student in the class must be made to understand that no one is above the other.

- A student with a physical disability is not below the child without limitation.

- A student who is from Asia or Europe is not better than a student who is black or from Mexico.

- A student who is LGBTQ is not lesser than a student who is not.

- A fat student is not less than a thin student.

- A student that comes from a wealthy home is not better than the student whose parents are from a lower socioeconomic status.

- A student from a divorced marriage is not lesser than a student whose parents are still together.

- A student that was adopted is not less than a student with his or her birth parents.

Educators can show movies that show the implications of those who think themselves to be better than others. Then, the educator should teach the students to always respect each other's choices and learn to live alongside each other intolerance.

REINFORCING EMPATHY

It is the job of the educator to always ensure children understand how to treat themselves. They are supposed to know kindness is a virtue that will help them grow into functional individuals in society.

EDUCATORS SHOULD KNOW THE PERIOD TO INTERVENE

It is vital for educators to understand some children would be impervious to the regular teaching the teacher tries to impact on them. Some kids have already been introduced to a cycle of manipulation and bullying from home, and this would make it difficult for them to change. Within families where children witness one parent abusing the other, a child may interpret the action to be the right way of relating with people. The child carries the dysfunctional mentality into the online atmosphere and begins to cyberbully other students. When such cyberbullying occurs, it is vital the educator intervenes in a constructive fashion.

First, the educator and some adults can isolate the cyberbullies and victim(s). Then, both sides would have to be questioned about the details of what occurred. At that time, the educator is to provide the emotional support needed for the victim while reassuring the victim such occurrences will be stopped. Afterward, the cyberbully should be taken to face the disciplinary measures set out by the school or handed over to law authorities. The educator must ensure this victim is reassured nothing will happen again at least from the same cyberbully. For instance, if the child is a victim of revenge porn posting, the educator should encourage the victim the compromising pictures or videos would not surface again. If the child was a victim of impersonation, assurances should be made to assure the victim his or her identity would be guarded thoroughly.

THE TEACHING OF EXPLICIT BEHAVIORS

Some educators fall into the trap of vagueness when teaching their students about issues such as cyberbullying. This is a pathetic reality because the incidence of cyberbullying is one that is destructive to the mental and physical wellbeing of children both in the present and future. In order to avoid falling into this pit of vagueness, educators must be very specific when telling their students of the kinds of behaviors they should prevent. Explicit cyberbullying behaviors should be stated include:

- The spread of rumors concerning classmates

- The act of joining websites that encourage cyberbullying activities

- The act of mentioning classmates explicitly or subtly on social media platforms such as Facebook, Twitter, Instagram, etc.

- The posting of intimate pictures of classmates and sharing of the same

- The act of making offensive comments on the profile posting of classmates.

- The act of filming their classmates without explicit permission granted.

- The act of posting pictures or videos online without the consent of the classmate.

All these and more are actions the educator must explicitly state to the students so they would quickly recognize any of such as cyberbullying. Repetition of this kind of class is vital within a school environment so the students will always remember.

REMIND THE CHILDREN THAT THE INTERNET NEVER FORGETS

School children who are often engaged in the act of bullying do not understand the long-term consequences of their actions. To them, the act of bullying other kids is just a mere passing activity that will be forgotten by the world. However, the educator should already know better. The educator ought to inform the students the first rule of the Internet is 'do not post what you cannot defend.' This is because nothing online is indeed deleted. Instead, they are archived in parts of the Internet where they can be retrieved in the future.

The teacher can bring up countless online examples of periods when the Internet did not forget the actions of certain people. In 2018, when it was time for the Golden Globe Oscar Awards, the comedian, Kevin Hart, was announced as the host of the show after a tremendously successful personal year. However, the Golden Globe Awards is a prestigious occasion which means people would scrutinize the history of the host. A scrutiny of the comedian's social media account dating back seven years revealed a tweet where he talked negatively about Gays. After the discovery was made, the LGBTQ community began to raise a campaign to have the comedian removed as the host of the show. After a sustained and successful attack, the host was dropped, and his reputation was affected.[70]

Students should be made to understand the Internet is accessible to every member of the public, and any act of cyberbullying will potentially hamper their chances of getting good stuff in the future. Also, bystanders that watch as cyberbullying occurs or chip in little offensive remarks are liable to having their reputation hurt in the future. While this kind of talk may not be too useful for some kids since they do not have the full logical capacity to think of the consequences of their actions, the teacher should not refrain from telling them.

TEACHERS SHOULD NOTIFY PARENTS OF THE EXPECTATION FROM THE CHILD

It is not enough for parents to be told cyberbullying acts in their kids are to be frowned at. The teacher must ensure the parent understands the full range of cyberbullying actions, especially the most recent ones. The reason is many parents do not have the luxury of time in getting information about the current trends of cyberbullying. Their child may be engaging in it without their knowledge. When the parents have an explicit list of cyberbullying behaviors, they would be able to curtail such acts within the kids.

EDUCATORS SHOULD OFFER REDEMPTION TO THE CYBERBULLIES

On a general note, many children do not like to disappoint their parents, teachers, and adults in general. That is why they strive to

---

[70] Bradshaw, P. (2018). The Kevin Hart Oscars debacle
https://amp.theguardian.com/film/2018/dec/07/the-kevin-hart-debacle-is-a-lesson-in-the-way-power-works-oscars

engage in actions that would earn them praise. When the educator discovers any cyberbully activity, it would be good to sometimes offer a chance at redemption. Let the bully or bullies win the respect of the educator by making right the wrongs committed.

The educator may offer a set of activities that can enable the offender(s) to be redeemed which may include engaging in volunteer service to a community, writing apology letters to the victim, learning about the pains being passed through by members of a demographic group, etc. The educator may end up discovering the child is remorseful for the previous action of cyberbullying.

SHOW FILMS ON BULLYING TO DISCOURAGE THEM

Since it has been discovered students learn fast through the use of film shows, schools have adopted it widely. At present, educators who are history teachers and wish to teach the history of the nation make use of films so the attention of the students are fully captured for the entire duration. The same tactic can be used in the quest for prevention of cyberbullying as films can spur children into making life-changing decisions to stop cyberbullying.

SECTION THREE:

Parents

Talking to Your Child Before They Are A Victim

Talking to children about bullying is an opportunity to make clear statements about what social behavior is acceptable and unacceptable. It allows parents to take advantage of teachable moments they can utilize to teach their children good decisions skills, reactions to the social deviations, and abilities in surviving the social space. It is this type of conversation that requires parents to plan efficient methods in talking about bullying with their children. It's part of the job for being a responsible adult in a child's life to talk about bullying, what it is, why it's damaging, hurtful and wrong, and how to withstand it, stop it, and avoid doing it.

Bullying is detrimental to both the bully and the victim. Research shows clearly there are potential psychological, social, and mental health problems that can damage relationships, welfare, and the wellbeing of both the bully and the bullied. Also, aside from the bully and the victim, there are third-party participant(s), the bystander. A child is likely to be one of these at some point. The best way to protect a child is to teach a child on everything concerning bullying. Also, by teaching children to speak out against bullying attitudes and by educating them on how to construct a peaceful society and friendships, parents are encouraging them to become more psychologically firm.

The following steps can be taken when talking to a child who might not know what bullying is, or hasn't experienced bullying before.

STEP 1 - KEEP IT GENERAL

The first point of conversation does not have to be made too formal or straight forward. Children are creative beings, and they tend to think in pictures. This is why creating a bullying scenario and asking them for their opinion works very well. Also, children tend to be overly expressive when they are doing what they find to be fun, so there is a need to pick the right moment to get the best response and outcome out of the child.

STEP 2 – TALKING TO YOUR CHILD

Talking to a younger child

The use of a picture book or the child's favorite TV show to illustrate what you are trying to tell him about comes in handy if the child is below the age of 9. This gives them an insight into how other people treat them and what to do when somebody makes them feel distressed. For example, let them know they can always talk to any of their parents or teachers. Streamline your talk and use scenarios the child can relate.

Talking to an older child

A child above the age of 9 years is old enough to handle real-life scenarios. Also, this set of children also get exposed to the internet to a higher degree, so there is a need to broaden the concept of bullying by teaching them about the different forms of online bullying, social bullying, and school bullying. Creating scenarios and asking the child how he or she will react is an excellent way to let he or she know the exact thing to do when they eventually find themselves in such a situation. It is also necessary children do not only get taught on how to react when they are being bullied, they have to be prepared not to be a bully and even to stand up against any act of bullying regardless of whether they are involved or not.

Every home must have specific technology guidelines and regulations. In addition to spending time online, teach your children online etiquette. It's just as simple as showing them to act as they would in real life. They must also not use a mobile phone or computer of someone else without permission, and they should not use anonymous or unrecognizable screen names to communicate the use of false or abusive language that might embarrass others without their authorization to circulate embarrassment or video about a person.[71] Teaching them this online etiquette will show them the ethics, and they will know when somebody is crossing boundaries especially a bully.

STEP 3 – KEEP TALKING (COMMUNICATION)

Talking to a child before they become victims should be a continuous activity. When children are engaged continuously on sensitive topics like bullying, it becomes easy to spot situations that might help them through any challenges they are having as regards to bullying. An active interest in their daily activities will give them a sense of assurance that they can trust you with anything happening in their lives. Ensure to keep up with knowing how they are feeling, get

---

[71] Brown, T. (2014). Cyberbullying: Online safety. New York: Rosen Publishing.

to know who their friends are, their online activities, and what they are up to in school. Keeping the communication open goes a long way in strengthening the bond that exists between parents and children, and it will go a long way in making them better social beings.

Make your child realize each story has two sides, and you will do your best to help your child if he or she is going through any phase relating to bullying. It is also good you ask about your child's friends if there is any case of a friend of theirs being bullied; encourage the child to persuade the victim to report it to the relevant authority.

Generally, children and young people are going to request assistance and advice in the face of problems if they happen to think their parents and guardians are interested and concerned about them. When parents spend some time each day asking their child what happened during the day and are genuinely interested in their experiences, they will know if they have a problem they can speak to their parents. Check in frequently with children and listen to them. Know their friends, ask questions about school, and get to know their concerns.

Working With Your Child After They Were A Victim

In cases when a parent suspects his or her child is being bullied asking the child outright may hinder communication, and so the child may not open up quickly. It is however essential that instincts be trusted as parents tend to sense when things are not right with their child. The child may not be ready to talk about whatever you want them to talk about but ensure an efficient communication line is established assuring the child he can talk about it anytime he wants.

If the child eventually gets to open up about being bullied, be sure to react with calmness; listen carefully then offer comfort and support. It is a fact kids always feel embarrassed and ashamed that they are being bullied, so they tend to hide it from their parents and the society at large that imposes responsibilities on them. Most are embarrassed their parents will overreact and make the issue worse. Sometimes they feel like it is their own thinking that just maybe if they had acted differently they wouldn't be bullied. Some get scared considering the bully will inflict pain on them if they found out that they told anybody. There is also the tendency a child will refuse to tell his parents because he is scared nobody will believe him.

It is therefore essential when a child opens up on being a victim in the past or the present, parents should take time to give them credit and praise them for doing the right thing. Because the term "bullying" is a broad term that encompasses different phases, no one-size-fits-all approach can be used. For example, the way different online bullying situations are handled is different from the way school bullying situations are handled. What will work for one location might not work in another situation. In most cases, however, teachers or counselors are the best people to talk to first. Sometimes children feel like they've done something to cause the intimidation., so telling an adult only increases their confusion and shame. Reminding the child bullying is the bully's choice is essential. Be sure your child knows he is not alone.

For some parents, it may be tempting to tell a kid to fight back. The urge to say to them to fight back will always be there, especially if you are worried the child will continue to suffer in the hands of bullies if they do not fight back. In some cases, children can and should be taught to stand up for themselves and for other students around them; however, getting into fist fights with bullies at school will only result in both students being suspended.

It is unfortunate, but zero tolerance policies at schools become an obstacle to standing up for oneself. I remember when I was in high school, I walked around the corner in the hallway only to be punched in the face by another student; it was a student I had never met and had zero prior interactions. He, the bully, was "just having a bad day." I was "in the wrong place at the wrong time." After his first punch hit me, he continued swinging, breaking my glasses and hitting me over and over. After a few seconds, I was able to forcibly push him back to get him off me; at that moment, a teacher stepped in and broke up the "fight." Even with security camera footage of the hallway showing I was a victim, the act of pushing him back was seen by the school administrators as I was fighting and both of us received a suspension from school.

When it comes to the internet, how will a child fight back against an anonymous profile on the internet that is continually frustrating their lives? How will they fight back body-shaming people who are far more physically attractive than they are?

In as much as there is no particular approach or strategy to talk to a child that has been a victim, there are some general strategies that will go a long way to put the child up and going again. One of such is to eliminate the possibility of future occurrences. If your child was bullied on an online platform, getting them off that particular social media platform may prevent similar events from happening in the future. But that is, of course, much easier said than done when the platform is massively popular amongst their peers. Arguments of "but everyone is on there" and "you just don't understand" will be common.

Also, teach them to be calm; it is natural for a child to get upset by the whole experience, but that is precisely what bullies thrive on. It makes them feel more powerful. Practice not reacting, crying, or looking red or upset. It takes a lot of practice, but it is a useful ability to keep off the radar of a bully. Sometimes it is helpful for children to practice "cool down" strategies like counting to 10, writing down their angry words, taking deep breaths, or walking away.

Ignoring the bully is by far one of the strongest weapons. If you can get your child to understand that as painful as it is right now, they must ignore the bully's comments and display an outward appearance of being happy. At first, the bully will increase their attacks, and your child should be ready for this. After they realize your child "just doesn't care" about their foolishness, the bully will move onto another victim.

Bullying can erode the confidence of a child. Encourage your children to spend time with good friends to help restore it. Taking part in clubs, sports, and other fun activities strengthens and builds a friendship. Allow your kids to tell you about the good parts of the day and listen attentively. Listen to your kids. Make sure they know you believe in them, and do what you can to deal with any intimidation that takes place.

Lastly, ensure that you assure the child you are on his side. This is a good measure as it will contribute to him regaining confidence, and it will act as a mitigating factor for the future occurrence of bullying. Get support from the right institution. If the bullying concerns a threat to life, the local police authorities should be involved. If it is a case of anonymous online harassment, it is essential you fish out the perpetrator by engaging the services of an investigator. However, if it is a case of school bullying, the school principal or school resource enforcement officer (SRO) should be notified, and if possible, the parent of the bully should be informed of their child's gross misconduct.

What to do when your child is the bully

Bullying can have tremendous effects on both the bully, the victim, and the parents of both sides. This is the reason why prevention should be the focus of everyone. It is usually tricky when parents discover their child is a bully. No parent ever wants to be called by the school to be told their child is a bully. This is why there needs to be some proactive actions taken to prevent its occurrence and reactive measures to bring the child to order. Whether the parents are together or not, it is more effective if they present a united front instead of one that is divided. Such division may be disastrous as the child may play it as an advantage. Here are some vital steps to take:

DO NOT BE QUICK TO DEFEND YOUR CHILD

Some parents choose to deny any accusation that their beloved little child could be a bully. It is vital parents understand their child may not be the saint they thought them to be. The child may have been given the best of moral education from the best tutors, taught spiritual lessons of tolerance ,and be a bright student, but none of these are guarantees the child would not become a bully.

Sometimes the child who becomes the bully is a product of a good home, sometimes a bad home. Socioeconomic and household status, while do play a part, are not guarantees of the child's outcome.

The appropriate course of action would be to engage in personal research to determine the true claims to the accusations. It is very possible your child is innocent, and it is also possible they are guilty. When the parents decide to blindly protect the child, the child may end up perpetuating more bullying under the shield that has been provided by the parents.

IDENTIFY THE ROOT CAUSE OF THE BULLYING

No action is ever taken in isolation. Your child did not begin to bully other children out of a single momentary impulse. There is something that may be eluding the parents and combined to push the child into the act.

A short list of possible causes are:

Marital Friction - This is one of the most popular root causes of bullying. When parents are undergoing stormy periods in their union, the children are victims that are forced to suffer.

Experience of being bullied - One of the reasons why a child may be a bully is the child may have been bullied in the past without receiving help. In some occasions, kids who have went through the experience when they are young often grow up to be adults that perpetuate the same cycle of abuse to others. Was your child a victim of bullying once? Was there any course of action undertaken to help your child? Answering these questions is vital, because it may be the reason why the child has decided to bully other kids.

Attention-seeking - Some kids decide to engage in bullying because of the care they try to get at the end. Such kids may be unpopular in their school and try to utilize bullying as a means of climbing up the ladder of fame. The results are usually favorable for these children as many kids seem to always gravitate towards the bully rather than the victim. When the parents discover that it is for fame, the child can be taught there are other legal means of gaining fame than cyberbullying.

Imitation - According to a group of philosophers, children are tabula rasa: blank slates that learn from copying everything within their environment.[72] When such children watch films portraying bullying, they may decide to take on the role of the bully. For instance, if a child attends a movie where one character uses bullying as a way of gaining power, the child may be motivated to use the same means in his or her real life.

After you have determined the root cause that pushed your child to the act, you will be able to proceed effectively.

REMIND THE CHILD THAT BULLYING IS A CHOICE

Educators and psychologists who have worked with children over the years have discovered many tend to shift the blame of their actions away from themselves. It is difficult for children to have a sense of responsibility at that period of their lives, and this is why the responsibility falls on parents to teach them how to be responsible. When the parent discovers the child has told the root cause of bullying, it is vital the child is told that bullying others was a choice. Despite the negative influences, other options were available for the child. Make the child understand that he could have chosen to be more kind

---

[72] MacFarlane, A. (1977). The psychology of children. London: Open Books.

towards other kids. The child could have decided to talk with the parents about a previous incident wherein the child was bullied. The child must be told to take responsibility for the action taken and on no account should the parents make the child feel the course of action was natural. Then, after the child has been entirely made to take responsibility, it is time to introduce the punishments because every choice made has either negative or positive reactions to them.

MAKE SURE LOGICAL CONSEQUENCES ARE DEVELOPED

Every crime has a punishment that comes after, and it is realistic if the punishment fits the crime. It is not enough for parents to merely talk negatively about bullying. Kids should be made to understand that the consequences are more than just a few words spoken against the act. The reason is this: every parent ought to raise the child in a way they will become functional members of the society in the future. Being a useful member means having a good knowledge of the rights and privileges of the citizen, as well as the laws that guide the society. Then, every valuable member knows the nature of punishment that is given when the rules are broken. If the parents refuse to punish the child with other means apart from words, the child will adopt a wrong belief that the judicial system dispenses punishments of a verbal nature alone.

TAKE AWAY PRIVILEGES

For teens mostly, the loss of privileges is a potent form of discipline that is widely adopted. Because this case concerns cyberbullying, parents can decide to take away phones, laptops, and other devices that can connect to the internet from the child. In this present age, many teens dread being completely shut out from the internet, and this makes the punishment to be more potent. Also, cutting away the access to the internet would stem the tide of cyberbullying. Other privileges that can be withdrawn from the child include:

- The restriction placed on the use of a car

- The restrictions placed on the availability of such child from attending parties and other special events

- Enforcing a rule to stay at home alone

When you are in the course of taking these privileges away, a united front ought to be presented by the parents, and no parent should cave into the child.

SUPPORTING THE DISCIPLINARY PLAN SET UP BY THE SCHOOL

Some parents often make the dire mistake of trying to speak against the disciplinary plans that are set up by the school in dealing with cyberbullying. The negative consequences of such action is two-fold:

- First, the school would not be able to establish a precedent that will be regularly followed. Every parent must always realize their child or children may be victims of bullying in the future. When kids within the school see their parents are united with the school, they would be discouraged from becoming bullies.

- Secondly, when a parent decides to go against the plan of the school, the child would be encouraged to go against the school rules more often. It would also create a dysfunctional mindset wherein the child would believe the only punishment that counts is the parents'. In the future, the child would get to realize the judicial system is not set up in a way that would allow the parents to have a say. It is essential the child sees the parents cannot speak for them every time. Mom and dad will not always be there to rescue the child from facing the consequences of actions taken.

TEACHING ANGER MANAGEMENT SKILLS TO THE CHILD

You can take advantage of a bullying episode wherein your child is the bully. In such an instance, you can teach the child anger management skills. Many children who are in their teenage years often express their anger in a negative pattern. You may decide to schedule your child for a visit to the therapist. However, you have a role to play in helping the child recognize constructive ways of dealing with anger. Part of the useful methods of managing anger for kids is to talk it over. The child should be taught the value of meeting the object of his or her anger and ironing issues out.[73]

TEACH SELF-ESTEEM SKILLS

If the root cause of the bullying was the child wanted fame, the parent should teach the child skills to improve self-esteem. Peer pressure usually thrives because of the desire of many kids to fit in and be loved by the majority. Hence, kids would engage in a series of adverse actions to be perceived as 'cool' by their friends. Parents should teach their children the benefits of having positive self-esteem. The child should be made to realize that her or his value does not come from people or other material possessions. Instead, the child should work to improve herself while not bothering to fit in. Parents should be able to teach the child that negative cliques are not helpful in the

---

[73] Bauman, S. (2015). Cyberbullying: What counselors need to know. Hoboken: John Wiley & Sons.

long run. Then, the child should be encouraged to develop healthy relationships with kids who are respectful of others.

SECTION 4:

Looking Forward

Lawmakers

A major challenge that arises for state legislators in the creation of cyberbullying laws lies in how the First Amendment guarantees the right of free speech for every citizen. However, the free expression of students does not guarantee them the right to interfere with or disrupt school discipline or activities. Their right to free speech does not also displace the rights of other students to be secure. This was made very clear in judgments such as *Tinker v. Des Moines School District*,[74] which first provided this limitation and *Nixon v. Hardin County Board of Education*.[75]

It is vital to note state laws are usually different from each other, as some states have chosen to regard cyberbullying as a criminal offense while others see it as a civil offense.

SUGGESTIONS FOR IMPROVED LAWS

Many countries across the globe have discovered the incidence of cyberbullying is detrimental to the whole fabric of society. They have noticed cyberbullying tends to create dysfunctional children who later turn out to be dysfunctional in the community when they eventually

---

[74] Tinker v. Des Moines Independent Community School District, 393 U.S. 503 (1969)
[75] Nixon v. Hardin County Board of Education et al, No. 1:2012cv01125 - Document 39 (W.D. Tenn. 2013)

become adults. Unfortunately, there have been little activities undertaken by many lawmakers who have legitimately refused to elevate cyberbullying from being a civil case to a criminal one.

This begs the question, where do we proceed from here in terms of the law? In providing quick suggestions to this question, it is better to recap the nature of cyberbullying itself and its effects to confirm if they are dangerous in life.

From the beginning of this book, our discussion of cyberbullying has been provided to refer to a series of bullying actions channeled against an individual or group through electronic/online means. Being it is a form of *bullying*, it is inherently devastating as it pushes an individual or group to destroy the mental health, physical wellbeing, and other aspects of the victim's life. In discussing the various effects cyberbullying brings to the victim, some chapters in this book have shown many victims suffer from issues such as reputation damage, increased risk of suicide, and other harmful effects. While some scholars still hold on to the assertion cyberbullying is just '*kids messing around,*' the statistics of teen suicide, drop in self-confidence, and reputation damage has shown problem warrants more thought by lawmakers.

Here are some suggestions that can be taken into consideration by lawmakers:

Developing a clear and nationally consistent definition on cyberbullying

Currently, the most significant barrier to lawmakers is different states formulating their definitions on cyberbullying. It is from the description of a particular legal issue that determines whether it would be viewed as a civil case or criminal one. At the moment, only a few states define cyberbullying as a kind of incidence that is criminal. For other states, the definition stops short of calling the act criminal, and this is why those states designate the school districts and schools to come up with disciplinary measures to deal with cyberbullies.[76] What are the key features that this nationally recognized definition of cyberbullying is supposed to have?

- An act of crime - the act should be defined as an act of crime that cannot be condoned.

- A bullying act committed through electronic channels

It is vital to note it would be difficult for all the states in the country to adopt a unified definition of cyberbullying; however, lawmakers can come to a general acceptance that the interpretation should criminalize the act.

Creation of uniformed educational materials

As stipulated by laws concerning cyberbullying, different states have engaged in the provision of separate materials to be used in the education of students, parents, and other personnel involved in the fight against Cyberbullying. However, one noticeable feature of these materials is they are not uniform in nature. For instance, states that criminalize cyberbullying with either jail time or fine, and sometimes both make available materials that speak more strongly against the incidence of cyberbullying. On the other hand, states which still maintain cyberbullying is a civil affair do not provide educational materials that exude powerful convicting language. This particular suggestion is very vital because educational materials go a long way in fashioning how children would think about the act of cyberbullying[77].

---

[76] Cyberbullying and the Law, Doe 464533 v N.D., 2016 ONSC 541 (CanLII).
https://www.canlii.org/en/on/onsc/doc/2016/2016onsc541/2016onsc541.html
[77] http://mediasmarts.ca/digital-media-literacy/digital-issues/cyberbulling/cyberbullying-law

For educational materials prescribed by states that have criminalized the act, cyberbullies would be taught that engaging in the act could potentially lead them to jail. Also, as regarding educators and other professionals within states that have criminalized cyberbullying, the educational materials would teach them to take more proactive actions in reporting cases of cyberbullying and also research on techniques to foster environments of tolerance within schools.

For states where cyberbullying remains a civil law, it has been discovered that students, parents, and educators have been a bit lax than the former. For example, in the case of cyberbullies, when they learn through the educational materials the consequences of their actions are suspension or expulsion, they would not be sufficiently afraid to discontinue the act. For victims, such educational content will not create solid trust in the school and state.

For parents of cyberbullies, such educational materials describe cyberbullying as a civil offense would not sufficiently motivate them to pay much attention to their children's activities.

Creation of regulatory laws on social media platforms to ensure quick prevention and prompt response

In the fight to curb acts of cyberbullying, many social media platforms have been lax, and this has safeguarded the continued practice of cyberbullying. For instance, within a social media platform like Twitter, users can post sensitive images and videos containing nudity. In this instance, it is easier for a cyberbully to engage in the posting of non-consensual revenge porn. Also, within the social platform, Instagram, users can quickly tag other users to a picture without the permission of the individual. Many cyberbullies have easily tagged the profiles of their victims to posts that are very offensive.

Another problem with social media platforms is the process of confirming the identity of any user is usually not stringent. This means children can easily create fake accounts which they can use in perpetuating their cyberbullying actions.

It is important to know these are some of the few lapses that are noticeable within social media platforms. To combat these deficiencies, states and federal lawmakers have to engage in the creation of fact-finding committees that would bring detailed reports on social media platforms. When these reports are eventually prepared, the lawmakers can call together vital stakeholders such as the founders of the social media platforms to consider on the kind of laws that would be detrimental to cyberbullying activities. After these considerations, lawmakers can propose laws that would make social media platforms safer for children.

CRACKDOWN ON REVENGE PORN SITES THROUGH LAWS

There has been reported progress in the crackdown on sites wherein revenge porn is posted. There is more work to be undertaken in terms of creating harsher laws that would discourage people from uploading revenge porn to such websites in the future. To ensure the incidence of revenge porn is quickly reported, such providers of porn must be made to display emergency phone numbers which can be used by victims of revenge porn posting.

Many other suggestions ought to be taken into consideration by both state and federal lawmakers in combating the incidence of cyberbullying. However, the major hurdle must be scaled is uniformity. Until all states lawmakers unanimously agree to criminalize the offense of cyberbullying, most of their efforts would not be as effective as they intend them to be.

INCREASING SCHOOL AND LAW ENFORCEMENT BUDGETS FOR IMPROVED TECHNOLOGY

When schools and law enforcement agencies have the proper budgets in place to utilize advancements in technology to help battle online predictors, revenge porn, and cyberbullies, the lives of all students improve. Awareness campaigns should include material easy to understand by parents, even those of limited formal educational backgrounds on how to use these services to assist in protecting their children.

Law Enforcement

What have been the roles played by law enforcement in curbing cyberbullying? This is the question to be answered when trying to determine the potential functions law enforcement can perform to reduce it. Recently, in a survey that was conducted by the FBI showed close to 82% of the officers believed cyberbullying is an urgent issue that warranted the involvement of law enforcement. The reason for the outcome is evident because of the acts of cyberbullying cuts across families across the entire country.[78] Children whose parents are Senators have been bullied, children of law enforcement agencies have been bullied, and the list goes on. It affects children of all walks of life.

However, the same study revealed that a particular demographic of law enforcement officers showed more interest in the issue. This demographic comprises of officers who come from minority groups, officers whose kids identify with being of different sexuality, and officers who have female children. The reason for this is the children of these officers have generally encountered incidents of cyberbullying more than others.

---

[78] How Should Law Enforcement Respond to Cyberbullying Incidents? (n.d.). Retrieved from https://www.stopbullying.gov/blog/2015/04/15/how-should-law-enforcement-respond-cyberbullying-incidents.html

Police intervention has been believed to be necessary within cases of cyberbullying because of the adverse outcomes that come from the act. On a general note, police officers have arrived at a consensus their roles cut across understanding the problem of cyberbullying to providing ways to combat it:

Understanding cyberbullying from a law enforcement perspective

Law enforcement officers have realized the first step to counter cyberbullying is to understand its nature. While many police officers already fully grasped the kind of physical bullying, many are struggling to grasp the nature of cyberbullying. If the state regards cyberbullying as a criminal offense, law enforcement officers would have more authority to enforce as opposed to states where it is considered to be a civil issue. Within all states, police officers are required to consult with the District Attorney liaison to know the existing criminal statutes that are applicable.[79] Cyberbullying issues such as stalking, coercion, posting of sexually explicit images as well as the sexual exploitation of youth fall under criminal law.[80]

Working with Others

Law Enforcement officers have been engaging in various collaborations with school authorities to combat the menace of cyberbullying. In many instances, the police officers act as guides that provide helpful information to the administrators on the power they possess in disciplining erring students. In such cases, the school administration may have conflicted with parents of both the cyberbully and victim. While the parent of the cyberbully may be pushing for

[79] How Should Law Enforcement Respond to Cyberbullying Incidents? (n.d.). Retrieved from https://www.stopbullying.gov/blog/2015/04/15/how-should-law-enforcement-respond-cyberbullying-incidents.html
[80] Police Training and the Problems of Cyber Bullying and Sexting. (2018, August 10). https://virtualacademy.com/police-training-and-the-problems-of-cyber-bullying-and-sexting/

more lenient measures to be taken, the parents of the victim may be pushing for harsher measures; this creates a dilemma for the school administration. Also, law enforcement officers have always advised school administrators as regarding some anti-Cyberbullying policies that can be adopted. With the officers acting in the role of advisers and potential enforcers, educators have made gains in ensuring children are taught the adverse effects and future punishments that come with acts of cyberbullying.

ESTABLISHMENT OF INTERNET CRIMES AGAINST CHILDREN TASK FORCE

In 2008, the *PROTECT Our Children Act*[81] was signed into law by the Congress. Being an abbreviation for *Providing Resources, Officers, and Technology to Eradicate Cyber Threats to Our Children*, *PROTECT Our Children Ac*t created the ICAC task force was to comprise of a national network of 61 coordinated task forces representing over 4,500 federal, state, and local law enforcement and prosecutorial agencies.[82]

On a continual daily basis, these agencies carry out proactive as well as reactive investigations plus prosecutions of people who have been involved in child abuse and child exploitation on the internet. The use among children and teenagers provided the spur for the creation of this organization which makes it essential people be discouraged from taking advantage of these children and teens. On the other hand, law enforcement agencies recognized making arrests would not singularly stop the occurrence of cyberbullying, and this is

---

[81] Providing Resources, Officers, and Technology To Eradicate Cyber Threats to Our Children Act of 2008 https://www.govtrack.us/congress/bills/110/s1738/text
[82] Marcum, C. D., & Higgins, G. E. (2011). Combating Child Exploitation Online: Predictors of Successful ICAC Task Forces. Policing, 5(4), 310-316. doi:10.1093/police/par044

why the ICAC task force is tasked with the responsibility of training law enforcement officers, prosecutors, and parents on the dangers of online activity for children and teenagers.

The scope of activities which the ICAC Task Force team covers is indicated on their website[83] and the body have to keep on playing increased roles in making sure more police officers, parents, and school educators are taught their obligations and how to effectively stem the tide of cyberbullying.

Combating cyberbullying does not only require the presence of laws and police officers, but it also lacks the creation of a systematic framework that would be used to investigate it. This framework is one that should be utilized by law enforcement officers, parents as well as educators.

However, it is important to state some tips and ground rules ought to be followed during this process of investigation.

ACT QUICKLY

This is the cardinal tip that all parties (parents, educators, and law enforcement officers) need to remember at all times. Delay is usually dangerous for every victim of cyberbullying because it increases the negative consequences that may arise from the act. For instance, the victim of revenge porn may show withdrawal symptoms in the first few hours or days of the incident and may commit suicide within hours of the bullying act. Upon suspicion that an incidence of cyberbullying is in progress, the educator, police officer, and parents should begin the investigative process and not leave anything to mere speculations.

---

[83] https://www.icactaskforce.org/

METHODS TO IDENTIFY THE CYBERBULLY

Asking questions

The second step of any investigation is to ask many questions concerning the issue at hand. In this instance, the educator would need to ask questions that include:

- What form of cyberbullying has taken place? Cyberbullying takes place through different ways such as websites, text messaging, emails, social media entries, photos, videos, and others.

- Who is the target? Is the target just an individual or a group of individuals

- Why is the victim being targeted? The investigator should identify the possible reasons why the cyberbully is targeting the victim. Does the child identify as an LGBTQ, or is the child part of the minority? Did the cyberbullying begin as a result of a fight between friends? Is jealousy rising out of competition? The investigator should be able to know this by asking questions from close friends of the victim. The investigator can also launch an inquiry into the motives of the cyberbully

- After identifying the reason why the child is being targeted, it is essential to know the nature of the cyberbully. Is the victim being impersonated online, or is the victim the target of negative rumors. Does it involve a threat of posting non-consensual revenge porn? The investigator can know this engaging in research into the online platform of the victim. Victims of non-consensual revenge porn postings are usually very secretive of the ordeal they are experiencing, and the victim may not be willing to tell their parents.

- When did the cyberbullying activity start? The investigator should chart the timeline for the period of cyberbullying.

Email Analysis

In this process, the investigator thoroughly analyses the email of the victim as well as finding a legal way to access the email of the suspected cyberbully. This is undertaken with the intent of evidence gathering. In engaging in this, the investigator can make use of various tools to get into the emails of the cyberbully and unwilling victim.[84]

Social Media Investigation

Every investigator of acts of cyberbullying must understand how to use social media platforms. This knowledge would be required to fully know the online activities of the victim and the cyberbully. The one benefit of the fact that the internet never forgets, and it is easy to retrieve any deleted information that contains evidence of cyberbullying. Furthermore, many social media platforms have teams that can be contacted to help with the provision of evidence to indict a cyberbully. These teams are also available to support the investigator in the removal of such content from the platform if the victim or the victim's parents are not intent on using the evidence.[85]

---

[84] Topcu-Uzer, C., & Tanrıkulu, I. (2018). Technological solutions for cyberbullying. Reducing Cyberbullying in Schools, 33-47. doi:10.1016/b978-0-12-811423-0.00003-1

[85] MacFarlane, A. (1977). The psychology of children. London: Open Books.

Cyber Bullying Investigations | Trustify - Private Investigators On-Demand. (2018, August 29). https://www.trustify.info/services/cyber-bullying-investigations

Made in the USA
Middletown, DE
18 July 2019